T0329751

The Sincerity Edge

THE SINCERITY EDGE

How Ethical Leaders Build Dynamic Businesses

Alexandra Christina,
Countess of Frederiksborg,
and Timothy L. Fort

STANFORD BUSINESS BOOKS
An Imprint of Stanford University Press
Stanford, California

Stanford University Press
Stanford, California

Special discounts for bulk quantities of Stanford Business Books are available to corporations, professional associations, and other organizations. For details and discount information, contact the special sales department of Stanford University Press. Tel: (650) 725-0820, Fax: (650) 725-3457

Printed and bound in Great Britain by
Marston Book Services Ltd, Oxfordshire

Library of Congress Cataloging-in-Publication Data

Names: Fort, Timothy L., 1958– author. | Frederiksborg, Alexandra Christina, grevinde af, 1964– author.

Title: The sincerity edge : how ethical leaders build dynamic businesses / Timothy L. Fort and Alexandra Christina, Countess of Frederiksborg.

Description: Stanford, California : Stanford Business Books, an imprint of Stanford University Press, 2017. | Includes bibliographical references and index.

Identifiers: LCCN 2017021825 (print) | LCCN 2017022150 (ebook) | ISBN 9781503603356 (electronic) | ISBN 9780804797450 (cloth : alk. paper)

Subjects: LCSH: Business ethics. | Sincerity. | Integrity. | Industrial management—Moral and ethical aspects.

Classification: LCC HF5387 (ebook) | LCC HF5387 .F678 2017 (print) | DDC 174/.4—dc23

LC record available at https://lccn.loc.gov/2017021825

Typeset by Thompson Type in 10.5/13 Adobe Garamond

To FREDERICK PAULSEN
His strong belief in moral and intellectual virtues
is a true inspiration.

Contents

Acknowledgments

The authors are grateful for a number of individuals and organizations who made the writing of this book possible, especially Jean Duvall, Associate General Counsel of Ferring Pharmaceutical, who has provided guidance and counsel to Countess Alexandra throughout her tenure on Ferring's Board of Directors. Jean also reached out to Professor Fort in 2009 to begin his working relationship with Ferring and the Countess.

Twenty CEOs and senior board members graciously took the time to complete our survey. We are grateful for their participation and insights, both to those who identified themselves to us and to those who remained anonymous.

The authors benefited from the work of many of Professor Fort's students. We have cited their contributions in the footnotes accompanying the relevant text.

Finally, the authors thank and acknowledge Kurina Fort for her assistance in preparing the index.

The Sincerity Edge

PART I

Foundations and Stories

1   What's Going On?

If a board of directors sought to improve a given corporate function—strategy, marketing, or human resources—where would they begin? A common starting point would be to benchmark what the company does against a set of "best practices."[1]

But what if "best practices" were not good enough? Ford Motor Company has long been a manufacturer of automobiles, but in recent years its board has realized that if they regard Ford as only a distributor of cars, it will not be recognized as a broader-based transportation company.[2] The Ford board now seeks best practices in terms of helping to design transportation networks for metropolitan areas, rather than best practices to simply make and sell more vehicles. A company's best practices thus depend on the template being used.

This analogy holds true today. Stakeholder demands—including those stakeholders called shareholders—press the agenda of corporate boards today very differently than they did, say, fifty years ago. Perhaps, as Norwegian investment banker Per Saxegaard argues, this is because the Internet provides a way for any interested party to have a voice, to capture a corporate indiscretion via a cell phone and immediately publicize it, and to organize a wide array of kindred spirits to put pressure on companies.

Companies need to make decisions about these issues. Are these decisions the domain of strategy? Philanthropy? Compliance? These issues could be called corporate social responsibility (or "CSR"), but even that name is unclear.

3

Practitioners and scholars differentiate among CSR, compliance, ethics, citizenship, shared values, and a host of other names for companies' efforts to adhere to obligations other than maximizing short-term profit. When people tire of the criticisms of one name, they adopt another term to shed the baggage of the first. Whether the effort is contributing medicines to Third World countries or instituting a values-based model of human resource management, we use terms such as *CSR* and *ethics* interchangeably because a larger issue lies at the heart of these semantic debates.

Why should businesses pay attention to ethical and social norms? Is it because they will make more money for the business in the long run? Is it because companies will be more likely to comply with the law or perhaps to obtain more leniency from a prosecutor or a judge given a company's conscientious history? Is it because people in a given company believe that integrity, trustworthiness, and authenticity have their own independent value worth pursuing?

These issues of trustworthiness, integrity, and compliance, as well as those of strategy, profit, and sustainability, are not new. They are the result of forces that have always affected companies. Some businesses ignore these forces; indeed, some of these forces can be minimized during certain times. Yet they do not disappear; a businessperson needs a template of these forces to navigate through what is going on today.

Drawing a Template

Illegal business behavior is not new, nor is unethical business conduct. As long as there has been trade, opportunities have existed for cheating. One need only look to ancient sacred scriptures to see the regulations and punishments set to deter cheating. Similarly, legal scholar Reuven Avi-Yonah has traced the notion of corporate social responsibility to Roman antiquity, arguing in part that governments provided companies with the benefit of limited liability in exchange for engaging in activities that benefited the public.[3]

Economists realize this as well. Nobel Prize–winning economist F. A. Hayek comments that if two people met in an isolated area, one party might kill or steal from the other; a person who could get away with it might just do that. However, to the extent that a community exists, sanctions will be imposed on the killer or cheater because it is not in the long-term self-interest of the members of the community to allow such behavior to occur. What is in their self-interest is encouraging productive behavior such as trading while discouraging killing and stealing. What fosters trade is for people to honor their promises, to tell the truth, to produce, and to sell high-quality products and services.[4]

It is arguably harder to pursue good virtues and profitable business today due to the rise of large business organizations combined with fluid global markets. Many commentators have noted that when management becomes separated from ownership, a new dynamic is introduced to corporate governance. A company with a dominant majority shareholder or a family-owned business will likely take on the values of the founder or owner(s).[5] In such cases, the differences between the leader's personal values and those of the company are not likely to be dissonant, and messages concerning appropriate behaviors will more easily flow through the organization.[6]

However, once companies undertake their initial public offering (IPO), the game changes. New investors enrich the company's capital structure (as well as providing cash for the founders). These new shareholders possess the same rights to voice their views as the company's existing shareholders with respect to how the company will govern itself. Many shareholders place a primary value on economic performance. At the same time, some companies do take steps to preserve their traditional way of doing business at the time of an IPO, and so some values—including noneconomic values—may persist in a company's culture over a long period of time.

A prominent example of this is the legendary case of Johnson & Johnson (J&J). When the company made its public offering in 1944, the founders attempted to perpetuate the company's (and founding family's) values through J&J's Corporate Credo, which set out duties and aspirations for the company, including service to, ranked in order, customers, employees, communities, governments, and finally to shareholders.[7] The company conducted training programs around the Credo for decades, making it a criterion for hiring and promotion decisions as well as daily conduct for J&J employees.[8] The pervasiveness of the Credo in J&J's culture was given significant credit for J&J's famous 1982 decision to remove its best-selling brand, Tylenol, from the dispensaries nationwide when an outside party sabotaged the product, resulting in six Chicago-area deaths.[9] J&J's CEO at the time, James Burke, explained that the company had to take such a drastic action because, without such action, "We couldn't live up to the Credo."[10] At the time, that unforced recall was considered to be a questionable business action tantamount to admitting guilt, but over time it proved to be a brilliant defense of the company's brand and its lead product.[11]

J&J's action proved to the public that it was a company that people could trust, keeping its products safe for the public and standing behind its promises. Tylenol had been J&J's best-selling product, producing 17 percent of the company's net income in 1981.[12] Two months after the recall, the company brought Tylenol back to the market with a market share that had plunged from 37 percent to 7 percent. A year later, the market share was back up to 30 percent.[13]

As admirable as J&J's commitment was, it is a difficult orientation to maintain in a publicly held company. Institutional investors, day traders, or individual investors using various mutual fund options are more likely to be interested solely in monetary returns.[14] Technology allows near instantaneous trading so that investors can move in and out of the market on an hourly basis.[15] That opportunity furthers investors' ability to evaluate companies on a very short-term basis. For such investors, monetary returns typically take priority over long-term strategies that emphasize values or corporate culture.[16]

In addition, investors from around the globe are likely to bring with them a diversity of values that may well challenge those that had been enshrined prior to a company's IPO.[17] And with 24/7 stock trading, the emphasis on ongoing evaluation of companies further enhances the importance of short-term monetary performance.[18] According to this template, honesty and integrity are not highly rated.

In spite of these pressures, the aim to create strong ethical cultures persists, as well as the aim for these companies to be perceived as having a social conscience. Even in the midst of these acute pressures for financial performance, evidence also suggests that ethical corporate cultures are correlated to economic success.[19] Lawmakers consistently pass legislation that attempts to rein in corporate excesses.[20] The public and civil society continually press for more responsibility and more social engagement. We will discuss the moral reasons for this throughout the book, but it is important to delve further into the economic reasons for why ethics is important to business leadership.

ETHICS EMBEDDED WITHIN ECONOMICS

Four leading economists provide examples of the argument that at the core of economics is a noneconomic ethical dimension that foundationally allows economics to exist and allows trade to develop.

Adam Smith is at the forefront of this supposition.[21] Smith, a moral philosopher, is most remembered for notions such as the "invisible hand" that creates social welfare even when "individual bakers and butchers" are acting from their own self-interest.[22] Yet Smith also argues that those individual bakers and butchers fill roles as citizens of a society with moral sentiments and obligations for the well-being of that community.[23] Businesspeople, in this light, are not *only* self-interested; they are also citizens concerned with obeying the law and being ethical.[24]

We have already introduced the Austrian economist F. A. Hayek, who took this connection a step further. Hayek argues that free trade benefits society in at least two ways. The first way pertains to how trade allows the production and accumulation of more material goods, creating a robust economy and the positive aspects that go with it (such as employment, better education, improved health).[25] Second, Hayek also argues that increased trade leads to international peace.[26] His argument is that trade creates relationships. Sustaining trade requires that those relationships be nourished by some straightforward ethical practices, such as truth telling, promise keeping, and the production of high-quality goods and services. This is one of the reasons that trade embargoes are so controversial. On the one hand, sanctions and embargoes provide a pressure point short of actual violence and so may provide the necessary pressures for changes without bloodshed. At the same time, the consistent lack of a trading relationship further isolates parties from each other, which may make subsequent peace-building efforts more difficult.[27]

A virtuous cycle can be created, Hayek argues, with parties recognizing that expanding trade requires such practices, which leads to more trade, which leads to a wider set of relationships, with a result that parties to a trading system will recognize both the value of sustaining the trade and also the ethical practices that sustain them. Both the trade and the ethical practices can logically lead to peace over war.

Part and parcel with the importance of trade, then, is ethics. Interestingly, Hayek's position does not inherently value ethics. He values ethics primarily because it allows for this trading matrix to develop.[28] Thus, his justification remains similar to that of the social welfare utilitarians, but Hayek delves deeper into the mechanics of the relationship. Hayek argues that the most efficient way for individuals to learn the importance of ethical practices is for civil institutions to teach such practices as having their own innate values; it is too inefficient for traders to learn this reciprocally supportive relationship through trial and error. Moreover, such inefficiencies mean that the knowledge gained will likely be after the fact and thus learned too late to benefit a particular exchange.[29]

A third example comes from the recent work of Robert Frank and David Rose. In his book *Passions within Reason*, Robert Frank argues that individuals make decisions on the basis of sentiments and emotion more than reasoned economic calculus.[30] He states that "[those] who are sensible about love are incapable of it."[31] Like David Hume before him, Frank recognizes that our emotions tend to be our first clue to what we should do, ethically and economically, and those emotions must be part of our understanding of both.[32]

Similarly, David Rose has recently argued that economics cannot create social welfare on its own (neither can the law, nor politics).[33] He emphasizes the need for ethics as a nonlegal, noneconomic discipline for restraint; guilt, he argues, can police aberrant behavior far more efficiently than economics or law and allows economic development to occur. As with the inefficiency and delay of learning the economic value of ethics through after-the-fact experience, guilt occurs too late to police behavior.[34]

Our view is that it is time to stop trying to argue that business can ignore ethical conduct and the society in which it operates. Whether a company is selling a drug, navigating offshore oil rigs, or running soccer tournaments, ethical conduct and being responsive to society matter. It is morally good for business to be ethical and socially conscious. It is also good economics and good for society. Simultaneously, businesses serve a social function—and behave ethically—when they convert resources into useful goods and services, the success of which is measured as a profit. Ethics and business are not an "either/or" issue; they are a "both/and" issue.

Today, it certainly seems that the public is increasingly intolerant of companies that seem to have little regard for society at large. In August 2015, Turing Pharmaceutical bought the rights to the drug Daraprim from Impax Laboratories for US$55 million. Daraprim is used in combination with other drugs to treat HIV patients; in the contract, Impax promised that it would remove Daraprim from pharmacies and wholesalers so that Turing possessed a monopoly on the drug. Martin Shredi, the CEO of Turing, promptly raised the price of Daraprim from US$13.50 to US$750 per dose, a 5,455 percent price increase, which instantly drew criticism from a variety of health-related organizations as well as politcians, including both Hillary Clinton and Donald Trump.[35]

Turing's experience is neither the most recent nor the first iteration of such issues. Years ago, the famed moral psychologist Lawrence Kohlberg penned a hypothetical vignette about a man named Heinz, whose wife was dying of cancer. The medicine cost the druggist US$400 to make, and he charged US$4,000. Heinz could not raise the funds to purchase the drug, and the druggist would not sell it for less, raising a host of ethical issues, such as whether Heinz should break into the druggist's business to steal the drug and whether the druggist was either coldhearted or believed that he could do more good for a greater number of people if he used his profits to create a bigger supply and wider distribution of the drug that would help more sick people.

More recently, the maker of the EpiPen, a medicine and injection system to provide emergency relief for someone suffering an allergic reaction, was found to have increased the price from US$249 to US$615 between 2013 and 2016, sparking outrage similar to Turing's experience one year earlier.[36] In contrast, Danish pharmaceutical Novo Nordisk has consistently won praise for its ethical conduct, including for its commitment to making its drugs available to everyone as a human right. This includes selling its insulin drug in Africa at no more than 20 percent of the average price in the Western world.[37]

After years of building its brand as "Beyond Petroleum," BP found itself involved in the worst oil spill in U.S. history with the 2010 Deepwater Horizon disaster. Public relations gaffes, revelations of unpreparedness, and lax safety issues undermined the company's reputation, and its CEO's complaint that he "wanted his life back" raised public concerns of the sincerity of the company's commitment to solving the crisis and its empathy with those affected.

Nonprofits are not immune from these troubles either. FIFA, the world soccer organization, has been embroiled in controversy for years ranging from the arrests of its leaders for violating bribery laws (related to the awarding of the World Cup venue to certain countries)[38] to violation of human rights standards in countries building facilities in preparation for the World Cup.[39]

With each of these, the public's outrage forced the organizations to react. Yet it seems that a better approach might be a long-term one in which ethical conduct is authentically integrated into company policies and sincerely practiced rather than reacting, after the fact, to a damaging scandal.

Many successful businesspeople do, in fact, see the positive connection between good ethics and good business. Although the news is often filled with scandals and outrageous businesspeople and their obsession with wealth and greed, it is at the same time not difficult to find leaders who agree with former Federal Reserve Chairman Alan Greenspan, who in congressional testimony stated that, in today's economy, reputation is the key value companies bring to the market; if they lose that reputation, this can end the company.[40] Greenspan's remarks came on the heels of the turn-of-the-century scandals of Enron and WorldCom and were made with particular reference to the demise of Arthur Andersen.[41]

One need not search long for examples of companies with a clear social commitment, such as Ben & Jerry's,[42] Whole Foods,[43] Timberland,[44] and many others. Such commitments do not ensure ethical perfection, but these companies do explicitly and conscientiously set out to integrate ethical values with their business models. Rankings of the most ethical companies also note large multinationals; Marriott, Pepsi, Deere, Henkel AG, Kao, Swiss Re, and Stora Enso, among others, have been recognized multiple times in *Forbes*'s annual rankings.[45]

In short, the integration of law, ethics, and economics is possible in business practice, and that possibility only heightens demand for concrete implementation of such integration.

These arguments find empirical academic support as well. In an exhaustive study of over eighty other surveys that attempted to measure the relationship between corporate financial performance and corporate social performance, Joshua Margolis and James Walsh found that there was a weakly positive correlation between the two.[46] That is, ethical conduct generally helps a company's profitability, especially when measured over the long term.[47] Companies can certainly be profitable without being ethical, but companies can also successfully integrate the two and even do slightly better financially when they do.[48] Other large-scale studies corroborate these findings as well. One can conclude that, on the basis of traditional economists, actual business practice, and academic scholarship, there can be a constructive connection between ethics and economics. Establishing that connection becomes critical for the creation and nurturance of a healthy corporate culture.

LEGAL REQUIREMENTS MANDATING DESIRED PRACTICES

The old adage that one cannot legislate morality seems to have fallen on deaf ears among legislators, who regularly adopt laws with very specific moral agendas.[49] This should not be especially surprising. Law and ethics may not be coterminous, but both seek to encourage certain behaviors and punish others. Although a central argument of this book is that the legal enforcement of moral values runs the risk of undermining the vibrancy of ethical corporate culture, the law does have a place in reining in unethical behavior. Many such regulations exist, and here are a few examples.

Europe's commitment to protection of individual privacy led to the passage of the European Union (EU) Privacy Directive in 2002.[50] The directive sought to protect EU residents from use of consumer data by businesses without their explicit consent.[51] More recently, the Data Protection Directive was enacted to provide further privacy protection pursuant to seven principles: notice to data subjects that data are being collected; the stated purpose for any use; the preclusion of data disclosure without the subject's consent; the security of stored data to prevent abuses; disclosure as to who is collecting data; providing data subjects access to their data with the right to make corrections to inaccuracies in the data; and making available measures for the subjects to hold data collectors accountable.[52] Both directives were enacted pursuant to the ethical objectives of protections of privacy and human rights.[53]

Another specific European example pertains to gender issues. In 2002, Norway introduced a proposal requiring women to hold at least 40 percent of executive board positions by 2008.[54] Similar legislation was then considered[55] and passed[56] by other countries as well. Here again, the laws were passed with the aims of promoting equality of opportunity for women as well as for human rights.[57]

Did these legislative efforts work? There are differences of opinion. Statistical goals were met in Norway, but some public companies delisted from exchanges to avoid having to comply with the laws. Our sense is that the lack of a definitive conclusion, however, will hardly preclude

additional legal efforts to achieve the normative objectives of a democratically elected legislature.

In addition to specific regulatory approaches, countries also adopt re-
flexive approaches to achieve desired norms. Two notable examples are the
1991 amendments to the 1984 U.S. Federal Sentencing Guidelines[58] and
Burlington Industries v. Ellerth, which was decided in 1998 by the U.S. Supreme Court.[59] These measures set out strong incentives for companies to
adopt internal policies to achieve ethical corporate cultures. In *Burlington
Industries*, the Supreme Court addressed issues pertaining to sexual harass-
ment, holding that a corporation could be held financially responsible
for the harassing activities of its employees. The Court also held that if
corporations had established good-faith practices to address complaints
and to train workers on what behavior was unacceptable, it could require
alleged victims to work through the in-house process before appealing to
the courts.[60] Similarly, the Federal Sentencing Guidelines offered reduced
financial punishments for companies convicted of federal crimes if the
companies had adopted "effective" compliance programs, including codes
of conduct, safe places for employees to make complaints, high-level internal oversight of the program, and self-reporting of violations.[61] As with
the European examples, the justificatory aims for these legal regimes were
grounded in ethical aims.[62]

AFFECTIVE DIMENSIONS

If making companies behave is dependent on law, then one could turn
to concrete notions of legal regulation rather than more ethereal notions
of ethics.[63] Robert Prentice has argued after the Enron and WorldCom
debacles that the antidote to such problems was not more ethics in business schools (though Prentice, a highly respected professor of business law
at the University of Texas, did not oppose such a proposal) but more law;
after all, he said, what happened in these turn-of-the-century scandals was
the flouting of extant law.[64] Similarly, Aneel Karnani, a highly respected
professor of strategy at the University of Michigan, argued in the *Wall
Street Journal* that ethics was not a needed topic in business schools.[65] If
ethics "pays," then strategy could easily handle its integration into business planning and perhaps do so better than philosophers.[66]

Perhaps it is, in theory, possible for corporate strategy or government
legislation to handle all ethical issues confronting business. To date, however, the record does not suggest that they do so in any comprehensive

way. Legislation perpetually reacts to the "scandal of the moment," and although such reaction may be quite valuable to rein in egregious behavior, the law does tend to be slow and overinclusive, thus requiring supplementation to be more effective. Moreover, the fact that Enron, WorldCom, and others flouted the law suggests that there was insufficient motivation to respect existing legislation.[67] Although corporate strategy may also be able to anticipate the market potential of moral sentiments, the record of quality management[68] and environmental management[69] tends to find their origin in noneconomic values that a social market asserts, in advance of an economic market finding a way to integrate the values into a business model.

We do not suggest that the study of ethics makes legislation and management irrelevant. Instead, we have proposed that these three be integrated, just as ethics and business themselves ought to be synthesized.[70] An essential element of such an integration is some degree of affection: a "sincere desire to do good." As we have already explained, economists argue that this element is necessary for economics itself to successfully function. We have argued for the efficacy of sincerity: that the optimal way in which ethics is effective is when moral actions are sincerely undertaken.[71]

Similarly, Harvard Business School's Lynn Paine has argued for the concept of organizational integrity.[72] Paine argues that employees simply are not motivated to comply with the law; one must build in aspirational quests—efforts to achieve ethical goods that have their own value independent of their profitability—to inspire them to attempt to reach the level of basic compliance.[73] Linda Treviño and Gary Weaver studied the efficacy of legal compliance programs and found that they worked when notions of procedural fairness, at a minimum, resulted in evenhanded application of the relevant laws.[74]

An Industry in Point: Pharmaceuticals

As contrasted in the different approaches of Turing, Mylan, and Novo Nordisk, do corporations manage themselves solely for the benefit of shareholder profit, or should they consider the well-being of other stakeholders? The pharmaceutical industry is an example of one where an integration of business success and social consciousness might fit together nicely. The industry is ripe with examples of companies attempting to execute a strategy to do just that. Whether they are successful is another question.

Hank McKinnel, former CEO of Pfizer, which has been subjected to significant fines and other legal action over the past few years, captured the essence of the pharmaceutical response when he said: "Because we have the ability to help in so many ways, we have a moral imperative to do so."[75] It is hard to see how they could not. Their very business is about making people's bodies, minds, and lives as a whole function better in a very real, concrete way. Nor is McKinnel's comment inconsistent with other companies in the industry, which through statements or policies extend their commitment even beyond consumer well-being. Johnson & Johnson, GlaxoSmithKlein, Novartis, Abbott Laboratories, and others have made similar commitments to the good of environmental responsibility.[76]

Actions seem to follow these pronouncements. Eli Lilly has been a major funder of "diabetes camps," in which children with type 1 diabetes are able to participate in traditional camp activities under the supervision of personnel equipped to deal with their issues. According to its February 13, 2013, press release, Lilly had donated more than US$20 million to these camps over the previous ten years and gives away much more to other projects. Much good has undoubtedly resulted from this action, and it should be recognized as good CSR, but, to put this in context, it is also worth noting that Lilly's 2016 revenues totaled over US$21 billion.[77]

Likewise, Bayer's 2016 revenues exceeded US$50 billion.[78] These revenues were ample to support drug donations such as the "Medicines for Malaria Venture," an organization created by the World Health Organization and financed by the World Bank,[79] as well as the United Nations Environment Programme to organize environmental projects every year for young people.[80] Its subsidiary, Bayer Cropscience, focuses on sustainable agriculture and has a program addressing African sleeping sickness.[81]

Following the same pattern, Pfizer's 2016 revenues of nearly US$53 billion provided ample cash to fund its "Diflucan Donation Program" (donating antifungal medication in sixty-three countries) and other programs.[82] The Lilly, Bayer, and Pfizer examples can be replicated. GlaxoSmithKline donates Albendazole as part of the company's effort to combat the tropical disease lymphatic filariasis, a leading cause of permanent disability and disfigurement.[83] Novartis donates multidrug therapy to all leprosy patients in the world through the World Health Organization, to date making contributions of more than 48 million packs valued at US$77 million that have helped cure more than 5 million patients.[84] AstraZeneca participates in a program focused on hygiene, infection, and reproductive health in New Delhi, India.[85] Boehringer Ingelheim provides free doses of a drug named Nevirapine to treat mother-to-child transmission of HIV.[86] Bristol-Myers Squibb launched a five-year US$100 million program in 2010 to fight type 2 diabetes in the United States and pledged an additional US$15 million in 2012 to expand the program to China and India.[87] Genzyme sponsors the Gaucher Initiative, a partnership with Project HOPE that provides the drug Cerezyme to patients with Gaucher disease who live in developing countries.[88] Abbott formed a public–private partnership with the government of Tanzania to strengthen the country's health care system and address critical areas of need, funding the program with more than US$100 million.[89] In perhaps the most famous public–private partnership, Merck has donated millions of dollars' worth of Mectizan to fight against and prevent onchocerciasis, also known as river blindness.[90]

Each donation may earn a press release touting the company's commitment to society, but does each press release carry the same weight? In other words, how can these programs be compared to one another, or even measured against each other?

These examples lay bare one of our central concerns and point to where pharmaceutical companies could aim better. Which is more compelling, a philanthropic program or a commitment to the integrity of a company? Philanthropic programs play an important role in society, but the level of commitment and their impact is often difficult to measure. The number of people helped and the number of dollars spent are presented as proof of social commitment, but it is difficult to know how to assess the company's true level of social commitment without the context of the number of people affected and the number of dollars earned. It is not that the philanthropic program is unnecessary; it is merely difficult to put into a measurable context. These are often stand-alone cases; because of that, companies can present such actions as evidence of how much they care while at the same time having such actions dismissed as window dressing by critics.

In addition to the difficulty of comparing numbers of people helped and dollars spent to revenues earned, CSR-as-philanthropy also makes "doing good" dependent on preexisting profit. This is an old criticism of CSR: A company can help only after it has first been profitable. Thus, profits come first and responsibility later. What does that do to responsibility during hard times? Is it passed over or discarded? Does such a model have any analytical basis in analyzing how profits have been made? If there is no model assessing these profits, could that then validate the claim that CSR-as-philanthropy really is just window dressing? These questions demonstrate that any kind of robust and sincere CSR must be more deeply embedded than philanthropy, even though philanthropy may be part of a robust strategy.

Philanthropic donations carry with them an appealing sense of altruism because of the equitable good done—treating children affected with worms, for example—but such donations are also vulnerable to the charge of window dressing because their impact is presented without context of dollars spent, revenues earned, and people helped. It is also sustainable only as long as the companies earn profits. Strategic CSR more deeply embeds practices that can address social issues—financial literacy and empowering those who do not use banking at all[91]—more sustainably exactly because the social issue is framed to help the company's self-interest. Yet, this appears to turn ethics into just another business strategy, on par with offering a money-back guarantee. Shouldn't ethics exist on a higher moral level? We seek to maintain the vibrancy of both philanthropic CSR and strategic CSR by articulating a paradox: The instrumental value of practicing virtues is at its highest when those virtues are practiced for noninstrumental reasons.

Why do firms engage in these activities? Marketing experts Kotler and Lee offer four reasons: it enhances corporate image; it feels good (which helps employee recruitment, motivation, and retention); it does good (increased market share or sales); and it has a lasting impact (increased appeal to investors and analysts).[92] Companies may not engage in these kinds of activities for all four of these reasons; a firm may simply see benefits from just one or two of them. Yet the four reasons raise two important questions.

First, do the benefits cited by Kotler and Lee come from these philanthropic engagements, or do they result from a more systemic corporate approach to responsibility? Corporate support of efforts to alleviate disease and improve sanitation should, one would think, help a corporate image. A boost in reputation may also have an impact on some of the other factors identified by Kotler and Lee, such as employee recruitment and increased market share and sales. But would such engagements really help in, for example, employee retention? We suggest that it would do so only if combined with other corporate actions that appeal to everyday concerns of employees, such as how they are treated and how they are empowered in their work.

Second, Kotler and Lee's four reasons beg the perennial question: Are these firms sincere in their efforts, or are their philanthropic efforts simply a public relations maneuver? This is not to demean good public relations, which are important to a company, or to suggest that companies must be wholly altruistic in their actions. Some degree of self-interest, of course, can be construed in any action. We are not suggesting that an ethical action is ethical only if that action shuns self-interest, but we do want to suggest that *the more a company and the individuals in it are sincere about a long-term commitment to doing good, the more their actions become trustworthy and beneficial to the company's instrumental consequences.*

For example, two people may begin to work together knowing that each brings something to a project they both wish to complete. Each has an instrumental trusting of the other because there is a readily apparent self-interest in treating the partner decently to achieve the agreed-on objective. If one of them becomes ill, the other might care for the sick partner simply because a healthy partner is more likely to be able to make the necessary contributions to the project. However, there is a higher level of trust if the parties are authentically concerned about each other's well-being, even beyond the instrumental goal of the particular project. That might make the healthy partner care for the sick one irrespective of the project. Again, the paradox is that the instrumental value of practicing virtues is at its highest when those virtues are practiced for noninstrumental reasons.

Stakeholders sense this as well. A company that engages in CSR activities as a slick PR move will not elicit as much value from those activities as if it is perceived as being sincerely interested in the activities. This is the fundamental, paradoxical complexity of CSR. There is more economic value when the economics are secondary to a higher moral or ethical motivation. Ultimately, then, a core question of any corporate social responsibility effort is whether the company cares. How does an artificial entity—such as a corporation—"care"? It does so by having a critical mass of individuals, especially at certain levels of the company, making it part of their personal identity and making it part of the institution's identity.

This argument is not as far from business reality as one might think. In a conversation with a high-ranking manager of the human rights/supply chain division of a Fortune 50 company, one of the authors asked what academics can do to help the manager in his work. The author assumed that the manager would want more empirical studies of how an action had more business payoff but was surprised to hear the manager say instead that he needed good stories of how a company can help people. "Anyone who opposes what I suggest can come up with a different number," he said. "But people still react to how company actions can impact other people."

In short, our argument is this: companies know there is value in looking good. Economics itself suggests there is value in integrating ethics and economics. Yet the biggest value—and today's leadership challenge—is to go beyond appearances and instead sincerely pursue responsible conduct as its own, independently valuable "good." It is then that ethical conduct has its greatest potential payback. That task requires more than words. Our book offers a process by which it can come to fruition.

Plan of the Book

Chapter 2 sets out a model for trust building and integrity in business. It argues that one builds integrity in three ways: hard trust, real trust and good trust. Our model of integrity and trust does not end the analysis of how business should conduct itself in the twenty-first century. Instead, it puts into leadership terms the persistent forces that are always at work in business and provides a model through which we can assess how and why some businesses fail and others succeed.

Chapter 3 uses these foundational perspectives to examine corporate scandals over time. It looks to explanations that have been provided for why they happen and also looks at how and why these scandals occur. From the first two chapters' framework of the forces affecting business, we examine how the companies failed to be trustworthy. This chapter draws heavily from our interviews with leading current and former CEOs and chairpersons and their observations of scandals. The chapter will also identify a number of key traits that seem to be associated with these scandals, with the goal of building a set of practical recommendations for how to avoid them.

In Chapter 4, we again use interviews with these executives and board members to examine examples of business behavior that have served as inspirational new ways of doing business. It looks to explanations that have been provided for why they happen and also looks at how and why these inspirational examples occur within the context of the opening two chapters' framework.

In Chapter 5, we look at making good decisions. Whether applied to strategy, ethics, marketing, or anything else, good decisions require being aware of our own inherent, cognitive biases, being analytical and methodical and gathering facts, applying the best knowledge we have to date and relying on our own intuitions and sentiments. This chapter provides a framework for making decisions with a particular emphasis on values-driven governance.

Chapter 6 argues both that sincerity is crucial for good, sustainable business conduct and that business conduct itself is most trustworthy—and most economically efficacious—if the conduct is both done for sincere reasons and perceived to have been done for sincere reasons. Chapter 6 contains illustrative examples of strong corporate culture. It explains why culture is a crucial determinant for values-driven leadership.

Chapter 7 serves as a capstone summary for the recommendations developed throughout the book.

We aim to show that sincerely pursuing ethical conduct is a good thing to do and is most effective (and also profitable) when done for these independently good reasons. We hope to lead business executives to reinforce this idea, and we will conclude with specific steps for the integration of ethics into business on an even deeper level than what many best practices currently carry out.

2   Integrity and Trust

What is the purpose of business? This threshold question has important implications for why sincerity is important and what it means for a business (and a business person) to have integrity.

A predictable response is that the purpose of business is to make money. Many people go into business—and remain there—to do just that: make money.

Yet it is not necessarily the reason why entrepreneurs *start* a business. Making money will be important to any businessperson, of course, but more typically there is also a *purpose* motivating a person to enter into business.

Whole Foods founder and co-CEO John Mackey asserts that he has never met an entrepreneur who started a business solely to make money. There was always an additional purpose. That purpose might be to prove to a parent that he or she could be successful, or to keep up with a sibling's success, or because the entrepreneur could not work under the authority of another person, or to provide ecological solutions that might thwart climate change. Mackey's point is there is always that "something else" that drives a businessperson.[1]

Norwegian investment banker Per Saxegaard agrees with Mackey. In an interview with the authors, Saxegaard also insisted that a start-up idea is typically purpose driven. Saxegaard describes a life cycle in which that purpose guides the conduct of the business until the business reaches a growth stage with professional management. At that point, the emphasis on efficiency and profit become stronger; if one is not conscious of the forces at play in emphasizing these quantitative elements, responsible behavior becomes more of a footnote. It is at this point, Saxegaard argues, that ethics issues begin to arise, whether intentional or not, and often are covered up until things explode in scandal. Then, the business enters the "sorry" phase in which it tries to get back to its roots.[2]

Johnson & Johnson, identified in the last chapter, is an example of Saxegaard's theory. A family company until its 1944 initial public offering, Johnson & Johnson was a purpose-driven company. In an effort to preserve that culture at the time of the IPO, the founders of the company created J&J's famous Corporate Credo, which detailed the responsibilities the company upheld.[3] Over the years, employees reported that the Credo and its values were very central to the life of the workplace.[4] In job interviews and in annual reviews, the importance of the Credo was reinforced, and sometimes annual rewards were provided to those employees who had the best story of the Credo at work.[5] This commitment was put to the test in 1982 when J&J was confronted with intentional outside tampering with its leading brand, Tylenol.[6]

Yet, over the past ten years or so, J&J's image has been tarnished by multiple product recalls.[7] Reports of the company's internal emphasis also have diminished, which perhaps might explain why a group of J&J shareholders filed a derivative suit against the company's board of directors for failing to perpetuate the ethical culture of the firm and thereby exposing the company to persistent legal problems.[8] In a settlement with the shareholders, the board committed to a stronger system of controls and checks to align the company with its original core values.[9]

Integrity is very much a holistic concept. Just as an integer is a whole number, and to integrate is to bring things together, integrity connotes a person or business that brings together and unites many virtues and forms of conduct. The difficulty is that the forces associated with professional management, globalization, growing the business, and other factors pull in different directions, placing great pressure on integrity. This, consistent with Saxegaard's corporate life cycle theory, not only increases the risk of unethical behavior but can also undermine basic trust in the company.

Major "whistle-blowing" cases since the turn of this century have focused on corporate cultures that have gone awry, including Enron,[10] WorldCom,[11] and the Bernie Madoff Ponzi scheme.[12] In the aftermath of the mortgage meltdown preceding the 2008 financial crisis, similar kinds of greed-driven cultures were reported within the financial industry, even among some high-ranking officials who reported that major institutions

sought to "rip the eyeballs out of their own clients."[13] The woes of some
pharmaceutical companies, such as GlaxoSmithKline's US$3 billion fine
for fraud in marketing several of its antidepressant drugs for unapproved
uses and for failing to report safety data on a diabetes drug, demonstrate
that problematic cultures reach beyond the financial sector.[14]

It is hardly surprising, then, that both practitioners and scholars focus
significant attention on issues of corporate culture. Such concerns with
culture extend beyond a desire to avoid scandal. From a business standpoint, there is widespread recognition that the culture of a company matters to business performance. To put it another way, integrity and trust
not only matter ethically; they matter as an issue of performance.

The realization that culture matters to performance has caught the attention of scholars. In their influential book, *Diagnosing and Changing
Organizational Culture*,[15] Cameron and Quinn provide a short case study
from the work of General Motors in the 1950s that demonstrates the
financial potential inherent in changing from a dysfunctional corporate
culture to one that is positive and constructive.

To avoid unionization, General Motors built plants in southern and
western states rather than in the more industrialized and unionized
northeastern and midwestern regions of the United States. This strategy,
not surprisingly, was frowned upon by the United Auto Workers Union
(UAW) and others, resulting in a highly conflicted work environment.[16]
The Fremont, California, plant with 5,000 workers who built the Chev-
rolet Nova model was particularly problematic; in 1982 the plant featured
low productivity, 20 percent absenteeism, and 5,000 filed grievances;
there were three wildcat strikes, and car assembly costs rose 30 percent
higher than its Japanese competitors.[17] Sales dropped, quality in its plant
was ranked worst, and customer satisfaction with the Nova "had hit rock
bottom."[18] Although the company had tried various strategies focused
on quality, human resources, incentives, and control systems, nothing
worked.[19] Finally, General Motors decided to partner with its competitor
Toyota to build a lighter car, offering the Fremont plant for the new automobile with a requirement that the plant was not to be remodeled and
that the old equipment was to be used. Toyota, for its part, was to hire
the most senior UAW workers (required because of a contract provision
related to joint ventures), which meant that the most alienated division
of the workforce would be used.[20] Toyota agreed, with the proviso that
Japanese managers would run the facility.[21]

The plant transitioned from producing the Nova to the Geo Prism and the Toyota Corolla, and the results were startling. Absenteeism dropped from 20 percent to 2 percent; unresolved grievances dropped from 2,000 to zero; total annual grievances dropped from 5,000 to 2,000; wildcat strikes fell from three to zero; assembly costs dropped from 30 percent above Japanese competition to the same; productivity rose from the worst in General Motors to double its average; quality rose from the worst at the company to the best, and the same result held true for customer satisfaction as well.[22]

Cameron and Quinn argue that although there may have been many reasons for the improvement, an interview with one UAW member summed up perfectly the reason for the change:

> This UAW member said that prior to the joint venture, he would go home at night smirking about the things he had thought up during the day to mess up the system. He'd leave his sandwich behind the door panel of a car, for example. "A month later, the customer would be driving down the road and wouldn't be able to figure out where that terrible smell was coming from. It would be my rotten sandwich in the door," he chuckled to himself. "Or he would put loose screws in a compartment of the frame that was to be welded shut. People riding in the car would never be able to tell exactly where that rattle was coming from because it would reverberate throughout the entire car. They never figure it out," he said. "Now," he commented, "Because the number of job classifications has been so dramatically reduced [from more than 150 to 8], we have all been allowed to have personal business cards and to make up our own job titles. The title I put on my card is 'Director of Welding Improvement.'" His job was to monitor robots that spot-welded parts of the frame together. "Now when I go to a San Francisco 49ers game or a Golden State Warriors game or a shopping mall, I look for Toyota Corollas in the parking lot. When I see one, I take out my business card and write on the back of it, 'I made your car. Any problems, call me[.]' I put it under the windshield wiper of the car. I do it because I feel personally responsible for those cars."[23]

Cameron and Quinn claim that the difference reflects a deep organizational change about how employees think about the company and their role within it.[24] To phrase it otherwise, purposefulness triggers the opportunity for integrity, and integrity entails trust. Without these dimensions, businesses can fracture, both in their conduct and in their performance. The two are interlinked.

These examples suggest that there are forces and trends that push companies toward or away from responsible business conduct. In this chapter, we suggest a template to take these forces into account. By doing so, we can better locate exactly where companies flourish in implementing responsible leadership, and where they falter. Locating these points will then provide the foundation for later chapters on how to make better decisions and how to foster more responsible corporate cultures.

Culture: Anthropology, Sociology, and Psychology

Cameron and Quinn's study of corporate culture has been very influential. The survey tool they use to diagnose cultural issues, called the "Organizational Culture Assessment Instrument," has been used by over 10,000 companies.[25]

Noting that there are more than 150 definitions of culture,[26] Cameron and Quinn summarize that there are two main approaches to the understanding of culture: organizations *have* culture (the more dominant, sociological view), and organizations *are* culture (an anthropological view), with a consensus that "the concept of culture refers to the taken-for-granted values, underlying assumptions, expectations, and definitions that characterize organizations and their members."[27] They state that "most people did not wake up this morning making a conscious decision about which language to speak. Only when confronted with a different language or asked specific questions about their language, do people become aware that language is one of their defining assumptions."[28]

Assumptions give rise to contracts and norms that govern human interactions in the organization, and they, in turn, give rise to artifacts, such as the buildings in which people work, the clothes they wear, and the kind of office they inhabit—as well as logos, mission statements, and formal corporate goals.[29] These then lead to the actual conduct of individuals in the company.[30] According to Cameron and Quinn, if one is to change culture, each level needs to be addressed.[31] They further argue that "culture" is more permanent than "climate," which "consists of temporary attitudes, feelings, and perceptions."[32]

The ethical climate approach to ethical issues in organizations comes from psychology and therefore emphasizes individual awareness, typically through strong leadership.[33] This results in focusing more on normative sentiments rather than anthropology's attention to structure.[34] Although we acknowledge the disciplinary difference, we believe that "ethical" corporate culture integrates analysis of corporate culture with the ethically oriented "ethical climate," so that the insights of both can be brought to bear.

THE COMPETING VALUES FRAMEWORK

Cameron and Quinn's research shows that there are four main types of corporate cultures: "clan, hierarchy, adhocracy, and market." The "clan" culture has a strong feeling of an extended family with the leaders of the firm seen as mentors or even parents.[35] Employees share a good deal of personal information at work, and this carries over to strong sensitivity to customers.[36] The focus is on long-term development, with resulting aspects of loyalty, cohesion, morale, teamwork, participation, and consensus.[37] Employee empowerment and open communications become crucial in this familial environment.[38]

The "hierarchical" culture, on the other hand, is very formalized and structured.[39] Smooth, long-term, efficient performance is valued, with leaders being viewed as coordinators and organizers.[40] Procedures, formal rules, and policies hold the organization together, and attention to employees focuses on secure employment and predictability.[41]

The "market" culture is a competitive results-oriented organization that tends to feature attributes of tough, demanding, hard-driven, and competitive people.[42] Winning motivates the participants, with success being defined in tangible measures of performance and market penetration; its leaders are hard-driving competitors.[43]

The "adhocracy" culture tends to be entrepreneurial and creative.[44] Its leaders are innovators and risk takers and encourage such traits in employees.[45] What binds members of the organization together is a commitment to innovation and a desire to be on the cutting edge, with success measured in the creation of new unique products and services.[46] In an innovative culture, creating new standards and finding creative new approaches become hallmark strategies.[47]

As with most academic typologies, Cameron and Quinn's framework is set out in an archetypical fashion, but they assert that any given business culture will be a mix of these four types.[48] The methodology to implement their research takes place in two steps. First, they administer a straightforward survey based on their research.[49] The survey is comprised of six questions (Dominant Characteristics, Organizational Leadership,

Management of Employees, Organizational Glue, Strategic Emphasis, and Criteria of Success), and respondents are given 100 points to allocate for each question among the attributes of the four culture types.[50] The survey is administered twice: the first time, participants are to answer the survey according to what currently exists in the workplace, and the second time the participants answer the survey according to what they would like to see in the workplace.[51] The difference between the two then provides a road map for how to make change and move from what currently exists to what is preferred.[52]

This question of change becomes very much the point. Cameron and Quinn name their approach the "Competing Values" model for good reason.[53] Values underlying hierarchy and stability exist in considerable tension with those emphasizing innovation, risk taking, and creating new standards. Similarly, tensions can be found in comparing these four types of culture and would be expected to continue as change occurs.[54] Yet, if one assumes that some kind of change is desirable, then it would seem that a value cluster committed to change is automatically elevated over others. Indeed, we would propose that the value cluster of "adhocracy"— the entrepreneurial, creative, innovative set of assumptions that seeks to set out new standards—would be the motivating value to balance among the three other quadrants, which otherwise seem to have little orientation to change per se. If this is true, then a reconceptualization of the framework accords with a tripartite model of nature and ethics.[55] William Frederick, a leading scholar in the field of business ethics relying on naturalistic foundations rather than on philosophical principles, has long argued that in all nature, there are three value clusters: "economizing," "ecologizing," and "power-aggrandizing."[56] "Power-aggrandizing" values are those that seek status and hierarchy.[57] They exist in the animal world, for instance with competition to become the dominant lion in a given pride or the dominant wolf in a pack.[58] "Power-aggrandizing" values also exist in the human world in quests for power and status; the corporate world is no exception.[59] Frederick tends to be quite negative in his assessment of power-aggrandizing values, because such individuals' quests for power and prestige can be very counterproductive to both economic efficiency and to community solidarity. However, they can have a stabilizing effect in the creation of laws and regulation that assure that rogue behavior is punished by authorities. This is the basis for the "trust" model of business ethics, which we will elaborate on further and which argues that individuals (and society) repose trust in a business when an outside party (typically the government through legislation) can prevent or punish egregious behavior.[60]

Frederick's "economizing" values refer to the naturalistic impulse to convert raw materials into usable forms. This also exists in nature, even in the plant world through photosynthesis and in the animal world through basic metabolism.[61] Frederick argues this process of converting raw materials into something useful describes what business does for society as well. Business, he claims, converts raw materials into usable products and services for society.[62] This naturalistic value maps well onto the economic approach to business.

Frederick's "ecologizing" values pertain to the long-term benefit of mutually beneficial relationships that give rise to the ecological system that allows life itself to flourish.[63] The entire ecosystem is based on these mutualisms, where one creature's existence is embedded within a series of other relationships with other creatures.[64] From the standpoint of human organization, Frederick argues that this is found in the communities in which we live as well, where mutual interdependence is crucial, a feature that fits well with notions of the affective.

Like Cameron and Quinn, Frederick argues that these are competing, mutually exclusive value clusters that present the challenge of how they can be integrated.[65] This is done, argues Frederick, in two ways. One is through what he calls "techno-symbolic" values that are simply our rational capability to recombine, restructure, and learn consciously how to adapt to new environments.[66] This capability is essential to our human nature and is the basis for everything from the creation of language to the design of complex corporate culture and nation states.[67] The other way in which these three value clusters come into some kind of relationship with each other is through what Frederick calls "x-factor" values.[68] These are the idiosyncratic features of individuals that spark change and differences in any given organization.[69] We argue that these are consistent with leadership and that the combination of leadership along with the human capability to reenvision, restructure, and change—a set of assumptions and traits that seem to map well onto Cameron and Quinn's Adhocracy Values—explain the culture-building map and opportunities for augmenting corporate culture.

In our reconceptualization, "hierarchy" would map with legal compliance notions of business; "market" would map onto the economic factors

Table 2.1. Comparison of leading corporate culture models as relating to Frederick's naturalist framework.

	Economizing	Ecologizing	Power Aggrandizing	Techno-symbolic/ x-factor
Competing values[a]	Market	Clan	Hierarchy	Adhocracy
OCI[b]	Satisfaction of needs	People	Security	Task
Denison[c]	Mission	Involvement	Consistency	Adaptability
Culture web[d]			Power Structures; Organizational structures; control systems; rituals and routines	Symbols; Stories
Culture map		Evidence values	Levers	Assumptions
Corporate evolution[e]	Systems		Structures	Technology; skills
Deal and Kennedy[f]			Process; tough guy/macho; work hard, play hard	Bet your company
Barrett[g]	Physical	Emotional		Mental; spiritual
Frontline[h]	Productivity rewards; rewards and recognition	Environment; teamwork	Objectives	Developmental opportunities for employees; leadership
Leadership Circle[i]	Task	Relationship	Reactive	Creative

of business; and "clan" would map with a moral dimension. Moreover, we believe that this mapping and conceptualization accords with a meta-analysis of other corporate culture templates that have been created. In Table 2.1, we take thirteen leading frameworks that assess corporate culture and ethical climate. Eleven focus on culture per se, and the final two address issues of ethical climate. As noted earlier, the differences between

Table 2.1. *Continued*

	Economizing	Ecologizing	Power Aggrandizing	Techno-symbolic/ x-factor
McKinsey 7S Model[j]	Strategy; Skills	Shared Values; Staff	Structure; Systems	Style
Ethical culture[k]	Rewards systems	Training; selection; fairness; informal norms	Rules; policies; decision processes; rituals	Leadership; stories; language
Alternate ethical climate[l]	Means to achieve goals; performance rewards; resources allocated to tasks	Relationship expected in firms		Determination of goals for the members of the organization

[a] See Cameron & Quinn, *supra* note 15.

[b] See Organizational Culture Inventory, Human Synergistics (Aug. 2014), available at www .humansynergistics.com/docs/default-source/product-info-sheets/oci_product_info_sheet_v1-0 _nopricing.pdf?sfvrsn=4.

[c] See Daniel Denison, *Denison Consulting*, retrieved on December 28, 2015, from www .denisonconsulting.com.

[d] See *The Culture Web*, MindTools.com, retrieved on January 2, 2016, from www.mindtools.com /pages/article/newSTR_90.htm.

[e] See *Corporate Evolution*, MindTools.com, retrieved on January 5, 2016, from www.mindtools .com/pages/article/newSTR_90.htm.

[f] *See* Terrence A. Deal & Allan A. Kennedy, *Corporate Cultures: The Rites and Rituals of Corporate Life* (1982).

[g] *See* Richard Barrett, *Barrett Model, Barrett Values Centre* (2009), available at www.valuescentre .com/culture/?sec=barrett_model.

[h] See Corporate Culture, *Frontline Learning* (2010), available at http://frontlinelearning.com /Corporate_Culture.html.

[i] See *Leadership Circle* (2014), available at www.theleadershipcircle.com.

[j] See *The McKinsey 7S Framework*, MindTools.com, retrieved on January 24, 2016, from www .mindtools.com/pages/article/newSTR_91.

[k] *See* Linda Klebe Treviño, *Ethical Decision Making in Organizations: A Person-Situation Interactionist Model*, 11 Acad. Mgmt. Rev. 601, 601–17 (1986).

[l] See Deborah Vidaver-Cohen, *Moral Climate in Business Firms: A Conceptual Framework for Analysis and Change*, 17 J. Bus. Ethics 1211, 1211–26 (1998).

the two tend to be downplayed when considered within the four-part framework for which we argue. The model captures much of the scholarship on the topic.

The rows across the top of Table 2.1 represent Frederick's value clusters. The column on the far left contains leading corporate culture and ethical climate frameworks. The cells then demonstrate how the leading cultural and climate frameworks use concepts similar to Frederick's model. What this chart shows is that there is a great deal of commonality vis-à-vis these frameworks, on the whole, and Frederick's model.

Another striking element is the emphasis that appears on dimensions around the final category, which pertains to leadership, motivation, desire, and aspiration. Although each category is consistently represented in the four cells, only this last category is featured in every cell; moreover, motivation appears to be emphasized more often than in the other cells. This suggests that the dimension of the affective—of leadership, x-factor values, and a working culture that is based on more than just compliance and economics—may be more crucial than any of the others.

Such an inference, of course, needs to be tempered by the fact that most of these analyses of culture are offered with an aim to change an existing culture.[70] Such an aim to change tautologically implies a motivation to do things in a different way. For that matter, even if only understanding, rather than change per se, drives a company to consider corporate culture, such an examination of corporate life has its value. Either way, the critical perspective of aiming for something better remains crucial to the creation of a preferred corporate culture or climate. This suggests that the affective dimension—an internally driven desire to achieve something—is essential for achieving an ideal (or at least workable) corporate culture.

So far, we have not suggested that one kind of culture is ethically preferable to another. A hierarchical structure has served the military for millennia, producing men and women of great rectitude, honor, and discipline. At those times when a company has spun out of control with many ethical or legal violations, it may well be that a hierarchical structure is necessary to impose the needed controls.[71] An outside market focus may be called for when a company's outlook has become too insular without regard for the variety of values existing outside the firm; this could be true when a company has failed to keep up with changes in the economic market or when it has failed to keep up with changes in the social or political market. A family-oriented business—one that is family owned, for example—may have been able to create an organization like an extended family, but such an organization may find it difficult to sustain that atmosphere as it grows and expands. An entrepreneurial firm may reach the point where it can become so entrepreneurial that it consistently eschews structure or bonds of relationship, creating a self-centered environment that may not even have a market payoff.[72] We believe that, for these situations, Cameron and Quinn simply identify their cultural change model as one of moving from an existing structure to a preferred structure.[73]

They are also, at the same time, saying much more than this. As their paradigmatic example, summarized earlier, shows, their framework provides a reminder that attending to issues of human pride, autonomy, relationships, and responsibility have both an independent value and a value in the creation of more productive workplaces. That message comes through in the analysis of other leading cultural change models, each one indicating the importance of the affective.

The Essential Dimension of the Affective for Ethical Culture

At the heart of ethics and ethical cultures are moral sentiments that feature a human quality: a caring nature for others. Some may characterize this as our human social nature[74] whereas others may go further and call it a moral aspect of our human nature.[75] Whatever characterization one makes of these natural sentiments, at the heart of any ethics—and at the heart of any change itself—is a desire to care about *something*.[76] And so, if there is a perception that a culture needs to change from a clan to a hierarchy or a hierarchy to a market, or any other variation, the sentiment of motivation becomes the starting point, immediately followed by the leadership and organizational capability to change.[77] Logically, this elevates "affective adhocracy" as the primary energy for change and an affective, clanlike approach as a substantively worthy model to aspire to. It also raises a significant challenge. What if the company is too big to be a clan? How does one maintain the personal caring aspect that typifies the clan paradigm when it is impossible for all employees to have direct contact with one another?

This is why John Mackey's insight is important.[78] There always is a second, noneconomic motive for starting a business. Mackey argues that the same holds true for employees as well, meaning that a key to success is to structure work so that employees have an opportunity to fulfill their desire for "something else" at work. In doing so, Mackey argues that great passion will be released and the company will be far more effective even as its work becomes more meaningful.[79] Such a model places significant power in the hands of employees, entrusting them to be mature moral agents.

To undertake the risk of changing an environment begs the issue of trust. There may be times and places where a company undertakes an action to gain good publicity and because of a perception that such a change will "pay." What makes those actions especially trustworthy, though, is when those actions are taken for sincere reasons committed to the good of the action itself, as opposed to the instrumental benefits that may accrue to the company.[80] Paradoxically, it is thus when actions are taken for their own good that they have the most value.[81] Moral sentiments, strategically developed and sincerely communicated, would arise from inside the organization, rather than be extrinsically required by laws and controls (associated with hierarchy) or through economic rewards (associated with markets). As a general rule, an optimal corporate culture would most likely be found in a clan structure with strong adhocracy practices.

That a hierarchically based or market-based culture may need to incorporate such virtues to achieve an ethical culture does not strike us as surprising. Hierarchy and markets—externally driven motivations—do not naturally engender affective sentiments and norms. Thus, to avoid stagnation, hierarchic and market-based cultures will need to find ways to allow for internally generated ideas and values. Cameron and Quinn state:

> Over time, companies tend to gravitate toward an emphasis on hierarchy and market culture types. Once their culture profiles become dominated by those lower two quadrants, it seems difficult for them to develop cultures dominated by the upper two quadrants. It is almost as if a law of gravity takes over. The lower quadrants have a tendency to remain dominant the longest. It takes a great deal of effort and leadership to make the change to a clan or adhocracy culture.[82]

Cameron and Quinn provide the General Motors example and transformation as indicative of the problem and the ensuing details of how it was solved.

Trust-Building, Integrity, and the Affective

There are governance implications for companies that seek to preserve a prized ethical culture while needing to attend to legal and economic pressures. External pressures associated with hierarchy and markets tend to grind against environments made up of empowered individuals making informed, independent decisions; once culture is driven by external pressures such as markets and laws, the culture tends to sag.[83] This suggests that conscious culture building must go into the creation of an organization right from the start.

For example, Kristin Hahn, a major Hollywood film producer, explicitly sets out to create exactly such an atmosphere of extended family when putting together a team to make a film. Hahn says, "We really look for people we know and whom we trust and who also will bring energy and fun to the film. Many talented people are available, but it's important to bring people together who can work together like a close community."[84]

As already set out, corporate culture is comprised of three forces. An entrepreneurial dimension—also known as a techno-symbolic aspect—is the force that blends the three, weighting as necessary to account for differences in size, type, geographical location, and industry. We propose that "trust" serves as an important value to integrate these three values in ways that are rule based, efficiency based, and community based.

HARD TRUST

The first type of trust we call "hard trust." Constituents may trust a company because a powerful third party makes it behave. That third party might be the government through its laws, or it may be public opinion. This is a crucial focus area for many pharmaceutical companies. Class action lawsuits, regulatory recalls of products, and other legal actions undermine stakeholders' trust in the company. There is a long list of stakeholders whose trust in a company might be undermined in a situation like Merck's Vioxx scandal, extending from consumers and regulators to employees and the general public. Vioxx, an arthritis medication manufactured by Merck, was linked to thousands of heart attacks. Its manufacturers, however, resisted a product recall until public and legal pressure finally compelled the company to withdraw the product from the market.[85] The first step for companies to protect their reputation is to address the issues in terms of legal compliance and negative public opinion.

Some pharmaceutical companies have been charged with exploiting local populations by conducting drug trials in nations where the regulatory apparatus is not as stringent as in the company's home country. These companies have been criticized for using direct advertising to consumers (as opposed to using care providers as the sole provider of information for prescription drugs) and for advertising that their drugs will address needs that they simply do not meet. For example, Bristol Myers Squibb was fined US$515 million after it was discovered that the company marketed its antipsychotic drug, Abilify, to treat conditions the drug is not officially approved for.[86] Similarly, in the largest settlement involving a pharmaceutical company to date, the British drugmaker GlaxoSmithKline pleaded guilty to criminal charges and paid US$3 billion in fines for promoting its best-selling antidepressants for uses not officially approved and also for failing to report safety data about a diabetes drug.[87]

Another charge made against some pharmaceutical companies is that they essentially bribe care providers. In June 2007, *The New York Times* reported that psychiatrists in Vermont and Minnesota topped the list of doctors receiving pharmaceutical company gifts and that this financial relationship corresponded to the "growing use of atypicals [new antipsychotics] in children." From 2000 to 2005, drugmaker payments to Minnesota psychiatrists rose more than sixfold to US$1.6 million. During those same years, prescriptions of antipsychotics for children under the state's insurance program rose more than ninefold.[88]

Companies tend to understand fairly well the need to avoid lawsuits and bad public relations, though they are not always successful in staying out of trouble. Especially in the aftermath of the enactment of the Federal Sentencing Guidelines (introduced in Chapter 1) and Sarbanes-Oxley in the United States, companies have been required to intensify their board oversight of compliance issues on a variety of fronts.

One might think that corporate codes of conduct should prevent many of these problematic actions from occurring. But every major pharmaceutical company has a corporate code of conduct, as does nearly every other major company (and many not-so-major companies). Codes of conduct do little, if anything, to actually prevent illegal or unethical behavior unless there is an authentic, sincere commitment to conducting business in an exemplary way every single day. Rhetorical odes to ethical conduct may even create a more cynical view of corporate responsibility if sincerity and actions fail to match politically correct verbiage. "Hard trust" works—codes of conduct work—when there is an aspiration motivating a quest for excellence (what we refer to later as "good trust").

REAL TRUST

Companies also might be trusted because good ethics can be good business, especially if measured over the long term. Many empirical studies show exactly that.[89] This is "real trust," and it occurs when a company takes care of its employees and customers—where it is honest, keeps its promises, and produces high-quality goods and services. This is an instrumental view of trust, and it is what tends to dominate in the business world and in business schools.

"Real trust" shares much in common with values-based management approaches. One of the authors has elaborated on this using a pharmaceutical company as an example.[90] Many companies invest heavily in training their managers to also be good people managers, managers who listen to their employees and help them maximize potential. There will always be situations that are not described in the company manual; therefore, it is preferable that management generates the company's values for employees and that employees take these values into careful consideration in the way they conduct themselves and their work on a day-to-day basis. This is an "empowering-of-managers" approach that corresponds to placing greater responsibilities on individuals and tapping into employee motivation and interest in learning.

Values-based training does not happen in a vacuum. If one seeks to integrate a values-based approach throughout a company, logic dictates that the most powerful elements of the company must be involved. This means CEO involvement. The old adage that ethics starts at the top is true, but if a values-based approach is going to be institutionalized, it cannot depend solely on the views of any one person. This means that an integrated approach must involve the board of directors as well as senior management. Just as compliance issues should have direct oversight by a board committee, so too should a values-based approach.

During the service of one of the authors on the board of directors of Ferring Pharmaceuticals, senior management at Ferring appointed an independent global ethics officer to take overall responsibility for ensuring that the company's philosophy, and the principles behind it were known and applied actively in all Ferring divisions. This work was organized in an ethics committee, which reports directly to the board of directors. The day-to-day work is carried out from the ethics office, and its remit is to disseminate awareness of these principles and values throughout the organization and to train and underpin each individual employee's integrity.

In many companies, work with ethical guidelines and compliance are consolidated into a single function and implemented through a common and coordinated effort. In such cases, the compliance function often has the greatest influence because it is easier to comply with something devised by a regulatory authority. Ferring separates the two functions of ethics and compliance so that both disciplines are worked on in parallel. By separating these functions organizationally but reporting the two together to a board committee, Ferring aims to place intense focus on the ethical component in its own right. It is important at Ferring that individuals are trained and supported in making the right decision in difficult situations.

The reputational advantages of a company's good works can create a "halo" effect that is beneficial for a company. A halo effect can give a company under scrutiny a benefit of doubt in a controversy. For example, the halo effect may have helped Merck after the FDA found that Vioxx put patients at a significantly greater risk for heart attack and stroke. Merck recalled its popular pain reliever and set aside US$4.85 billion in potential fines along with an additional US$1.9 billion for legal costs.[91] The chair of the U.S. Senate Finance Committee, Charles Grassley, argued that the FDA was "more than passive" in holding Merck accountable; a leading cardiologist from the Cleveland Clinic went further: "The FDA didn't do anything . . . they were passive here."[92]

Such regulatory passivity may have many reasons, but Merck's reputation and aggressive public relations and legal campaign reduced the estimated judgments to less than 10 percent of what had been projected.[93] This became no more than a short-term hit to the company, especially as new drugs were introduced to the market.[94] Merck recovered financially, reporting US$47 billion in gross revenues by 2012,[95] slightly less than its 2011 gross revenues of US$52 billion. A crisis of such magnitude might arguably deal a more crippling blow to a company.

Focusing on reputation, however, may not be as advantageous as focusing on the good that results from sincerely taking people's lives seriously. Companies deal regularly with pressures to increase sales and reduce costs. These pressures are especially urgent in the short term, particularly at a time when long-term economic benefits (like reputation) are difficult to quantify. If a company seeks to establish a good long-term reputation, some other value needs to be present to help companies through short-term pressures and to keep them trustworthy.

GOOD TRUST

This leads us to "good trust." This exists where there is an authentic concern for others. This sincerity recognizes business realities, but it also recognizes that there are many things that motivate people. "Good trust" taps into a part of human nature that makes people genuinely want to be proud of what they do.

One key way is through the values-based empowerment methods described in the previous section as "real trust." This demonstrates the point we have been making throughout this chapter. A senior manager who seeks to empower someone lower on the corporate ladder needs to convey an authentic belief in the capabilities of that person, or the empowerment may fail. Sincerely believing in another person complements the message of empowerment.

This is a crucial point. For ethics to be practiced and embedded in a company, there must be an important core of sincerity. Thus, "real trust"—like "hard trust"—requires a huge degree of sincerity to be effective.

Conclusion

From what we have seen, corporate culture depends greatly on an affective dimension to be effective. External pressures may have their place—companies, after all, do interface with societal markets and laws—but there remains a crucial intentional commitment to the good of ethical values that empower individuals and make culture a living force for good decisions as opposed to a reaction to pressure. It would seem, therefore, that a key component to a strong ethical culture lies in a commitment to virtues having their own independent value. We tested this hypothesis directly with twenty-one leading executives known for the ethicality of their businesses, and we describe their insights in the next two chapters.

3 Corporate Dilemmas in the Absence of Integrity and Trust

When presented with a program aiming to build integrity and trust in the entity, the head of a major U.S. government agency said to one of the authors, "I have thought and thought, and, for the life of me, I cannot think of a connection between leadership and ethics."[1] No wonder the agency had just experienced significant ethical lapses.

Unfortunately, the agency's director seems to have company. The landscape is littered with institutions—both governmental and private—that have experienced ethical scandals to such an extent that the term *business ethics* is often laughed off as an oxymoron or a short subject.

Yet Jeff Fettig, CEO of Whirlpool, suggests something quite different when he says that the expectation of integrity, ethics, and trust is the norm at his company and for many other companies with which he works. The scandals tend to be more the exception than the rule.[2]

We agree with Fettig, although remaining keenly cognizant of the number of corporate scandals that undermine confidence in business. In this chapter, we will show what key business leaders have to say about leadership and ethics and also what they highlight as some of the worst behavior in business. In juxtaposing these two points, we will show key reasons why businesses lapse into scandals; how we know that they are, indeed, inappropriate; and how the road map defined by these leadership methods themselves helps them to understand good business behavior and the leadership that can build long-term integrity and trust.

What's Going on Now

Asking businesspeople what they think about ethics and leadership is nothing new. Some trace an important start to the current academic study of the topic to a survey conducted by Father Raymond Baumhart, then dean and later long-time president of Loyola University in Chicago. In the book *An Honest Profit: What Businessmen Say about Ethics*, Baumhart surveyed businesspeople to capture their values and to see how they made ethical decisions.[3] Baumhart wrote:

> Ours is a business-centered society. No group in America is more influential than businesspersons. Their influence, for good or evil, enters every life and every home. . . . If it is judged business is corrupt, then it will be assumed that society is corrupt.[4]

Baumhart's comment from 1968 seems to be as applicable today, not only to the United States but throughout the world. Capitalism has different faces, but, on the whole, the world has adopted a market-driven approach stretching across the continents. One cannot underestimate the influence of business, and so the values of business leaders remain vital.

COMPLIANCE TRENDS

An important way that companies integrate values into daily business life can be through corporate compliance programs. Sometimes these programs result from a noble leadership commitment to conducting business in a way that values employees, customers, shareholders, suppliers, the environment, and the community alike. At other times, these programs result from a need to keep government regulators at bay and to prevent lawsuits from being successfully filed. Although the second reason is not the most inspiring rationale, it can also serve as a starting point. And if companies begin at this starting point, the evidence shows just how much they need to take on to run these programs well.

Indeed, advising companies how to do this has become big business. Consulting organizations, such as the Corporate Executive Board,[5] track trends associated with these compliance programs. Although our aim is to push beyond compliance programs per se, they do provide a starting point for the questions we posed to executives. Running a biennial survey since 2004, the Corporate Executive Board summarized five trends from these surveys.

First, compliance programs and staffing varies according to industry. The more a company is highly regulated, the more compliance is likely to be independent of other functions such as human resources or a general counsel. For example, in 2010, 71 percent of pharmaceutical companies had independent compliance programs, whereas 85 percent of telecommunications compliance programs were housed under a legal department. Not surprisingly, this suggests that a key reason for these programs lies in the need to respond to regulatory demands. Yet, on the whole, legal departments tend to dominate compliance programs less than in the past. In 2004, legal departments controlled compliance programs 70 percent of the time, but that control shrank to 58 percent by 2014.[6]

Second, the scope of compliance activities has grown and become more sophisticated. The programs have evolved from a past emphasis that ranged from traditional code of conduct development, staffing helplines, training programs, and effectiveness measures to newer functions such as monitoring third-party controls, reviewing potential new partners, risk management, and undertaking internal investigations.[7] If compliance programs possess a significant legal function, then why do the parties associated with this function increasingly come from outside the General Counsel's Office?

Third, boards of directors have become more engaged in the overview of compliance programs, especially with respect to audit and governance committees. Indeed, in the aftermath of the turn-of-the-century corporate scandals, boards increasingly have come to see compliance oversight as central to their responsibilities. Legal liability and regulation, of course, strongly influence and encourage such engagement, but our interpretation is that members of boards also see that such engagement is crucial to the company and to their duties. This makes it more important for a board to have specialized knowledge so that its members can assess issues of legal compliance and ethics as well as auditing per se. Or, to respond to that government executive who saw no relationship between leadership and ethics: boards of directors see the exact opposite. Their leadership is crucial.

Fourth, there are more compliance liaisons or ambassadors whose work is to make the compliance programs more accessible and understandable to all employees. Top to bottom understanding of the programs is, again, driven by legal requirements,[8] but for reasons we have already seen and will discuss later (for example, increased transparency resulting from the rise of the Internet), companies also see that lack of employee understanding can quickly reflect poorly on a company's global image.

Fifth, there is a trend toward a more holistic view of program effectiveness. These include tests or feedback results from internal and external sources. Interestingly, the Corporate Executive Board's research shows that "strong levels of corporate integrity at an organization help profitability, employee engagement, and productivity levels and overall risk reduction."[9]

This result lies at the heart of our argument. What makes integrity so important? Each of these findings by the Corporate Executive Board reveals that the legal component remains important, but the reality—not idealistic dreaming about ethical conduct, but the business reality—is that to achieve effective compliance, more than the law is required. Companies recognize that the holistic notion of integrity includes obeying the law but also presses further to include leadership, engagement, communication, and several other traits. Together, these make for more effective programs.

Yet, as important as this realization is, it simply shifts the question. Companies may see that integrity goes beyond the law and is helpful in complying with the law, but does that mean that companies embrace integrity because it simply is a superior economic strategy? Is integrity's importance driven by its utility, or does it have independent value? Or, as we will suggest, does its utility depend on that independent value? Moreover, who are the people on the board or in the executive suites who can adequately lead in the oversight of the teaching of company values and the evaluation of the company's success in each employees' learning of those values?

WHAT EXECUTIVES TOLD US

Without disparaging the compliance function, which is crucial in any business, we sought to look at the values that might nudge an organization, its leadership, and employees to concern themselves about compliance in the first place and also to understand the values that executives themselves saw as crucial dimensions of integrity and trust.

We surveyed twenty individuals who currently are or recently have been chief executive officers and/or board members of major companies. Approximately half of these leaders are based in northern Europe and half are in North America. Seventy-five percent of them lead companies with more than 500 employees. The leaders come from a wide variety of industries ranging from pharmaceuticals to manufacturing to shipping to the film industry. We asked these leaders to identify examples of ethical scandals (which will be reported later in this chapter) and also to identify examples of exemplary ethical behavior (which will be reported in the next chapter). We also asked them questions about corporate culture, which we will discuss in Chapters 5 and 6.

We then asked them a series of questions about the values that are important to their companies. For example, we asked what the most important drivers are for the ethics in their companies. Eighty percent said that legal concerns are important or very important; the same percentage also said that reputation and morale are important or very important. Perhaps more interesting, however, was the result that showed that 95 percent of those surveyed said that the most important driver in making ethical decisions in the company was that it was simply the right thing to do, and 100 percent said that being ethical served as a competitive business advantage.

We also provided them with a list of commonly approved virtues and asked whether these virtues were very important, important, neutral, not very important, or not at all important in building trustworthy ethical cultures. On a weighted scoring, presented in Table 3.1, the most important virtues were honesty, integrity, accountability, sincerity, loyalty, and resilience.

Next, we asked who in the company has a significant voice in setting the values of the company. Not surprisingly, all the respondents named the CEO, with 95.5 percent identifying the board and approximately 88 percent also identifying the founder of the company. Human resources accounted for 70 percent, and the general counsel's office produced 5 percent.

Finally, we provided twelve factors that would be important in creating and sustaining a positive ethical culture. Weighting the responses, the executives told us that the most important were:

1. "Tone at the top"

2. Supporting the company's values even when they appear to cost the company money, at least in the short term

3. A long-term focus

Table 3.1. Most important virtues as determined by surveyed CEOs.

	Very important	Moderately important	Neutral	Moderately unimportant	Very unimportant
Honesty	100.00% 20	0.00% 0	0.00% 0	0.00% 0	0.00% 0
Loyalty	40.00% 8	50.00% 10	10.00% 2	0.00% 0	0.00% 0
Sincerity	52.63% 10	47.37% 9	0.00% 0	0.00% 0	0.00% 0
Integrity	95.00% 19	5.00% 1	0.00% 0	0.00% 0	0.00% 0
Accountability	75.00% 15	15.00% 3	10.00% 2	0.00% 0	0.00% 0
Creativity	25.00% 5	30.00% 6	30.00% 6	15.00% 3	0.00% 0
Humility	15.00% 3	45.00% 9	20.00% 4	20.00% 4	0.00% 0
Efficiency	20.00% 4	40.00% 8	20.00% 4	20.00% 4	0.00% 0
Ambition	15.00% 3	55.00% 11	20.00% 4	10.00% 2	0.00% 0
Resilience	50.00% 10	25.00% 5	25.00% 5	0.00% 0	0.00% 0

4. Clear, well-understood policies and goals

5. Listening to all stakeholders

6. Matching employee rewards and incentives with company statements of values, objectives, and aspirations

7. Leadership's articulation of why daily actions make a difference to the well-being of the larger world, beyond the company itself

8. Continuous seeking of new ways to make the company and its culture better

See Table 3.2.

Table 3.2. Most important factors as identified by surveyed CEOs.

	Very important	Moderately important	Neutral	Moderately unimportant	Very unimportant
Tone at the top	95.00% 19	5.00% 1	0.00% 0	0.00% 0	0.00% 0
Listening to all stakeholders	50.00% 9	33.33% 6	11.11% 2	5.56% 1	0.00% 0
Long-term focus	65.00% 13	15.00% 3	15.00% 3	5.00% 1	0.00% 0
Clear, well-understood policies and goals	50.00% 10	45.00% 9	0.00% 0	5.00% 1	0.00% 0
Active engagement of the board of directors	30.00% 6	40.00% 8	25.00% 5	5.00% 1	0.00% 0
Matching [company rhetoric and employee rewards]	45.00% 9	45.00% 9	0.00% 0	10.00% 2	0.00% 0
Outreach in addition to, or instead of, financial philanthropy	15.00% 3	35.00% 7	35.00% 7	15.00% 3	0.00% 0
Standing behind values despite perceived cost	85.00% 17	5.00% 1	10.00% 2	0.00% 0	0.00% 0

With a survey of this size, we do not claim that our survey passes tests of statistical significance, nor do we claim it randomly surveys business leaders. Indeed, we have focused our study on these executives because they have a preexisting reputation as being solid, ethical business leaders, and so these results may well be skewed. If we were to ask a broader cross-section of leaders, some of whom do not think ethics is important, virtues of honesty and integrity might not score as highly as they did in our result. There will be other times and places—there already have been—in which scholars and consultants undertake such surveys. Our interest has a narrower and, we think, deeper scope.

Table 3.2. *Continued*

	Very important	Moderately important	Neutral	Moderately unimportant	Very unimportant
Giving employees the opportunity to share stories of ethical work behavior	35.00% 7	50.00% 10	15.00% 3	0.00% 0	0.00% 0
Giving employees the opportunity to share stories of unethical work behavior	35.00% 7	55.00% 11	10.00% 2	0.00% 0	0.00% 0
Small work groups/teams enabling individuals to experience the daily consequences of their actions.	0.00% 0	35.00% 7	35.00% 7	30.00% 6	0.00% 0
Leadership's message about positively affecting the world beyond the company	50.00% 10	35.00% 7	15.00% 3	0.00% 0	0.00% 0
Continuous striving for improvement	55.00% 11	30.00% 6	10.00% 2	5.00% 1	0.00% 0

Our question is, if a businessperson thinks that ethical leadership is important, then exactly what virtues seem to help the most? Which stakeholder voices seem to be the most important based on the experience of those leaders who are already committed to the ideal? What factors seem to help in creating positive, ethical cultures? Asking such questions requires a preselection of those who have commitments in this area, and we readily acknowledge an inherent bias toward the importance of ethical leadership. Most important, however, is how to undertake such leadership well.

We also want to know if the identification of these factors, virtues, and stakeholders provides a lens through which we can analyze the times and places where corporate scandals have occurred. Our view is that if we know the virtues and values from ethical business leaders, we have a better chance of being able to more precisely pinpoint what causes scandals and how to avoid them. In the end, we will show that among these values lies the importance of sincerely pursuing ethical conduct.

Thus, we also asked the leaders for examples of unethical behavior in business. They replied with the following examples, which we will summarize in the next section: Enron, Ford/Firestone, GM/Toyota, Martha Stewart, BP, and Lehman Brothers.

Before providing synopses of each of these cases and analyzing them, there was a seventh example that requires consideration. Environmental sustainability is, of course, a very important issue. Companies regularly tout their environmental consciousness, but one of the respondents took a dim view of the entire green movement, at least insofar as it relates to business:

> I believe that sound companies need to build profitable businesses on the basis of capitalistic, market-based healthy business models. If there is no natural demand driven way to achieve profitability and they instead have to rely on and lobby for public funds, this is in my opinion unethical. It is also damaging to society and the economy as a whole, as money used to support economically unsustainable businesses must necessarily come from healthy businesses that could have created sound investments and jobs much more efficiently. So for me, e.g., much of the green energy industry is completely unethical, relying on misleading politicians and consumers about the value proposition of their products in order to achieve personal benefit at the cost of other, much more rational and ethical business people.

Although this is not a position we endorse, there is a logic to the respondent's view. If one takes a pure, or relatively pure, free market system and takes resources from a business that "wins" by the free market rules and moves them to a business that does not, then there seems to be an unfairness. This is particularly true if, as the respondent writes, the claims made by some proponents of green business are misleading. Even aside from misleading statements, on the whole, this logic applies to a good deal of "corporate welfare."

It strikes us, however, that the respondent's position is more of a public policy question than one of ethical business leadership because the decision to allocate resources from a business that "wins" to one that does not results from a governmental decision of what industries to promote. Even given this, we would argue that governments have been favoring one industry over the other for centuries, and we generally support the efforts of government to promote green companies. Nevertheless, we do want to acknowledge the logic of our respondent's position.

If we are going to ask leaders what they think, then we have an obligation to avoid cherry-picking answers that suit us. Thus, we will focus on actions and culture-building steps that build trust and integrity as business people and business institutions while recognizing there is robust debate on public policy issues concerning public support of various industries.

The Stories Behind the Examples of Corporate Troubles

The examples we provide in the following subsections are, for the most part, well-known.[10] We present them here because the executives cited them as being examples of problematic business conduct. Our aim is to reprise the cases and then to match them against the values identified by the executives.

ENRON

If the Johnson & Johnson 1982 Tylenol recall is the corporate poster child for a company that made the right decisions in a time of crisis, Enron probably takes that role for a company that did everything wrong. In the 1990s, Enron was much admired. The company was formed in 1932 under the name Northern Natural Gas Company and was headquartered in Omaha, Nebraska. The company grew out of the modest Midwestern culture of Warren Buffet's hometown, and in 1979 it was reorganized as a subsidiary for a holding company called HNG/InterNorth Inc. New CEO Kenneth Lay moved it to Houston and changed the name of the company first to Enteron before shortening it to Enron.[11]

In 1990, Lay hired Jeffrey Skilling, who had been a consultant from McKinsey, to become chief operating officer. Skilling in turn hired Andrew Fastow as chief financial officer.[12] From there, the Enron story has been well chronicled. Enron moved aggressively to exploit a newly deregulated energy market by building power plants and natural gas pipelines. The company used its increasing leverage to garner high prices for its energy; for example, it was implicated in intentionally withholding energy from California in 2001 to create "brownouts" to obtain higher market prices.[13] For six consecutive years in the 1990s, *Fortune Magazine* named Enron a top innovative company.[14] In 2000, Enron's revenues amounted to US$100.79 billion with a market capitalization of US$70 billion.[15]

The company also pioneered "innovative" accounting methods based on a "mark to market" method. Under this method, the company would record income for a contract based on an estimate of their future value, discounted to net present value. This itself was not particularly new, but with very thin data as to what the value of their energy products would produce in some of their newer lines of business, the determination of those future values were difficult to support and tended to be arbitrarily determined in favor of Enron's balance sheets and revenue statements. As a result, actual income lagged.[16]

Inevitably, this created debt, an issue that the company had struggled to deal with long before its 1990s "innovations."[17] Andrew Fastow's answer was the creation of special purpose entities that, at least in theory, allowed Enron to move debt off its books and onto the balance sheets of these other entities. Though Enron ultimately remained responsible for these debts, moving them "off-shore" made Enron's official balance sheet appear robust.[18]

Maintaining the viability of the company with this precarious financial structure resulted in constant misinformation and fraud by Enron's senior executives. As one hedge fund manager once said to Skilling, "You are the only financial institution that can't produce a balance sheet or cash flow statement with their earnings."[19] Among charges later filed against various Enron executives, the U.S. Department of Justice indicted Skilling on thirty-five criminal charges, Lay on eleven counts, and Fastow on seventy-eight counts.[20]

Although we will have more to say about Enron's culture in Chapter 6, one example of Enron's shenanigans may be useful. Pursuant to Enron's code of ethics, an officer or director of the company could not own one of the special purpose entities (SPE). These SPEs were funded with 3 percent equity. The opportunity for an owner of these SPEs was to cash out the equity and leave only debt on the SPE's books. The cashing out of the equity would allow an individual to reap significant cash.[21]

According to the Powers Report, a report of independent directors of the company, Fastow desired to have an ownership interest in these SPEs. So as not to violate the company's code of ethics, Enron's board of directors formally suspended its "code" three times. During each suspension, the board gave Fastow the ownership interest he desired and then reinstated the code. Thus, Fastow obtained his ownership interest (and cash), and the company could say that it did not "violate" its code of ethics (because the violating action occurred while the code was suspended).[22]

Eventually, Enron collapsed. Even as it did, Enron executives continued to reassure both public investors generally, as well as employees who held shares of the company, that all was well with the company, even as the same executives liquidated their own holdings ahead of the eventual bankruptcy.[23]

MARTHA STEWART

Just a few years after the Enron debacle, the U.S. government filed charges against an iconic American figure: Martha Stewart. Indeed, the actual transaction that led to her indictment and conviction occurred in the midst of the Enron meltdown. Although Stewart's insider trading charges did not have the magnitude of national or global impact on markets of the Enron situation, the contrast of Stewart's scandal with her wholesome celebrity status jarred the public.

Stewart's mix of family-oriented entertainment and the securities market had a long history. She grew up in New Jersey, and, after graduating from college, she worked as a stockbroker in a small Wall Street firm from 1965 to 1972. She simultaneously worked on the decorating, gardening, and homemaking skills that would make her famous, and in 1976 she launched a catering business. In 1990, she partnered with Time Publishing Ventures to publish a monthly magazine, *Martha Stewart Living*; in 1993, she began her television show and also created merchandising relationships with stores such as Kmart. Given the success of these ventures, she bought out Time Warner's share in her business and created Martha Stewart Living Omnimedia (MSLO) in 1999, with her company's stock listed on the New York Stock Exchange.[24]

Stewart's felony was more in a personal role than as leader of MSLO. However, with criminal charges pending against her, and given the entangled nature of her and her eponymous company, the company suffered.

When news of the investigation became public, the stock of MSLO dropped 25 percent overnight; a month later, the stock had lost more than 50 percent of its prescandal value. Because of this entanglement, Stewart and other MSLO executives faced a shareholders' derivative suit as well as a class-action suit for shareholders' loss of value.[25]

The nine charges against Stewart concerned her trading on a tip from an advisor from Merrill Lynch, Peter Bacanovic. Bacanovic had left a voice mail message for Stewart on December 27, 2001. Less than four hours later, Bacanovic's office sold Stewart's entire holdings of ImClone stock.[26]

The insider trading aspect of the case hinged on the question of whether Bacanovic made his recommendation to sell ImClone stock because of financial analysis and publicly available information (which, of course, does not constitute insider trading) or whether it was because ImClone CEO, Sam Waksal, knew that the company had failed to obtain FDA approval for a promising drug, Erbitux; before that news became public, Waksal told friends and family to liquidate their shares. In fact, Bacanovic, who was also Stewart's broker, assisted Waksal's daughter in selling $2.5 million of ImClone stock the same day as Stewart, suggesting that the insight for the "sell" recommendation was derived from insider information.[27] By selling her stock before the FDA news became public, Stewart avoided a loss of $45,673.

In response to the charges, Stewart claimed no knowledge of any insider information, insisting that she had previously issued a put order that would require sale of the stock should it dip below $60 per share. Additional evidence, however, did not support this claim, and investigators uncovered evidence that Stewart and Bacanovic engaged in re-creation of data after the charges were announced that amounted to obstruction of justice.[28]

The significance of all of this, of course, could be minimized as an example of someone who simply was caught violating securities law. But Martha Stewart was not just an anonymous investor, and so her personal activity—here in terms of stock trading—had a direct impact on the company itself.

LEHMAN BROTHERS

Five years after Stewart's court case, Lehman Brothers initiated another financial/stock market fraud that helped plunge the country—and a good part of the globe—into the worst financial crisis in eighty years.

In 1987, the Federal Reserve (the Fed), under the leadership of Alan Greenspan, lowered the reserve ratio that banks must meet in the aftermath of the "Black Monday" market collapse.[29] The Fed furthered an easy monetary policy in the aftermath of the September 11, 2001, terrorist attacks, and along with the 1999 (effective) repeal of the Glass-Stegall Act, which allowed financial institutions to conduct both investment and commercial banking, the stage was set for the creation of massive financial institutions.[30] In the subsequent competition for capital, some institutions invested in mortgage-backed securities and other collateralized debt obligations that were often further dependent on the growth of the subprime home loan market, many of which had low introductory interest rates that could adjust upward over time.

When the housing market turned sour and rates increased, home owners began to default on their mortgages, which undermined both the repayment of debt and the collateral supporting the debt. This had a direct impact on firms such as Lehman Brothers, which had become the primary dealer of these mortgage-backed securities.[31] In, 2007, Lehman posted profits of $4.2 billion. With a stock price of $86 per share, it had a market capitalization of nearly $60 billion.[32]

But when the stock market began to plunge in 2007 and as the real estate market also spiraled downward, mortgage-backed securities started to fail. Though the executives at Lehman continued to claim that the company was in solid financial condition, the downward spiral jeopardized the entire existence of the company.[33]

Chief financial officer Erin Callan and CEO Richard Fuld Jr. devised a plan to disguise Lehman's disastrous situation through a technique internally known as "Repo 105." Under the plan, Lehman assets were sold to a phantom company called Hudson Castle at 105 percent of their value. Hudson Castle appeared to be an independent company but was actually controlled by Lehman. The assets were then repurchased by Lehman a few days later. Pursuant to accounting rules, the repurchase could be treated as sales, and this therefore removed them from Lehman's balance sheet, transferring/hiding nearly US$100 billion.[34]

Later, the company's global finance controller admitted there was no substance to the Repo 105 transactions and the use of this technique was concealed from ratings agencies, the board of directors itself, and from investors. Lehman's auditor, Ernst & Young, did not report the dishonest activities either. Ultimately, the company was in dire straits. In July 2008,

Lehman had claimed that it had $40 billion in liquidity but three months later admitted that it only had $2 billion in easily liquefiable assets. Its stock had fallen to only 6 percent of the value it held eight months earlier, and the company filed the largest bankruptcy in U.S. history.[35]

FORD/FIRESTONE

In the late 1990s, insurance companies began to piece together evidence that indicated there was a serious problem with Firestone ATX tires on Ford Explorers. One representative of State Farm Insurance company, one of the largest auto insurances in the world, reported twenty cases of the problem from 1992 through 1998 and then found thirty additional cases in 1999.[36] The National Health Traffic Safety Administration began to investigate; by late 2000, it had found evidence of 103 deaths, 400 injuries, and 2,200 complaints. Extending back further and prior to the issue arising in the United States, documentation showed similar issues in warm-weather countries such as Venezuela and Saudi Arabia, and Ford replaced Firestone tires on more than 46,000 vehicles.[37] Internal memos at the time showed that Ford employees had concerns that Firestone was withholding evidence of a "problem" with its tires.

In August 2000, Firestone recalled 6.5 million tires, with priority given to customers who lived in the warmer southern states in the United States.[38] According to Ford, the data provided by Firestone showed that there was a problem with several of Firestone's tires, particularly those manufactured in a plant in Decatur, Illinois.[39] The rate of damage from the tires made in Decatur was ten times the rate of one of Firestone's other facilities making the same type of tire.[40]

In the investigation that followed, both Ford and Firestone came under considerable pressure. Investigators asked Ford why, with knowledge of the problem in other countries, the company had done so little to prevent the problem in the future. The answer from Ford CEO Jacques Nasser was that there were no available data from countries such as Malaysia, Saudi Arabia, and Venezuela; what the company knew was simply anecdotal.[41]

The company was also faced with allegations from Firestone that claimed that part of the problem was the SUVs themselves. Given their top-heavy construction, SUVs, including the Explorer, were prone to roll over, thereby causing injuries. Had the construction been safer, the argument went, the cars would not have rolled over so easily after tires blew out. Investigators also learned that Ford's 1990 tests—presented to

Congress in claiming that the Explorer was safe—were not done with an Explorer, but with a "mule"[42] (or preproduction vehicle and not the actual model vehicle itself). Ford responded that the tires in such a test "think that they are mounted on an Explorer."[43] In other words, even though the car tested wasn't the actual car, the pressures placed on the tires via "the mule" would be the same as on an Explorer.

Despite these problems, critics generally praised Ford for its response because it provided a thousand-person team to handle customer calls and to investigate the cause of the problem.

Much more criticism fell on Firestone. At the heart of the problem were tires that were falling apart, creating an enormous safety issue. Firestone, like Ford, knew of the problem before the case erupted in the press, but Firestone claimed that driving conditions in Middle Eastern countries, like Saudi Arabia, were "extreme and unusual."[44]

That plausible explanation, however, did not explain the problems at the Decatur manufacturing plant, where 40 percent of the recalled tires were manufactured and where the tire creation process was primarily based on workers building tires manually.[45] After a strike at the plant, the company tried to catch up with customer demand by implementing a seven-day-a-week work schedule with twelve-hour shifts. Workers complained about the schedule, saying that it was difficult to do quality work under such conditions. Poor process control and nonstandard operating procedures were also cited as problems.[46]

Furthermore, Ford had fewer problems with non-Firestone tires on its "Explorer" than it did with Firestone tires. Other automobile companies had more problems with their Firestone-provided tires than they did with tires provided by other manufacturers. This provided strong evidence that there was, indeed, a problem with the quality of Firestone tires.[47]

The impact on Firestone was significant. In additional to product liability lawsuits, sales for the company fell dramatically with both unsold (defective) tires and a damaged reputation making new sales much more difficult to achieve.[48]

GM/TOYOTA

Our CEO respondents also identified the recall problems of the world's two largest automobile manufacturers, Toyota and GM, as examples of companies that became sidetracked. GM's issues revolved around an ignition switch; Toyota's concerned a "sticking" accelerator. Both resulted in traffic deaths.

Drivers reported that GM cars could suddenly shut off when driving. When that happened, air bags would not inflate in a collision, and neither power brakes nor power steering would work. According to records, the company had known about the problem since 2005, but the company had done nothing about it.[49] Based on an internal GM email, some have alleged that GM decided that it was cheaper to pay the expected warranty costs of ten to fifteen cents per vehicle than to fix the problem for ninety cents a car.[50] In 2007, GM did decide to correct the problem for new vehicles, but it did not recall older cars with the same problem. However, when they did fix the problem for the new cars, GM did not assign a new part number, which made it almost impossible to tell whether or not a car was fixed (and, whether this was intentional, also made any legal prosecution more difficult to maintain).[51]

In 2014, GM began announcing recalls of up to 800,000 cars for this problem, and, within a few months, it had also issued forty-five separate recalls for 28 million cars worldwide, some of which related to airbag malfunctions that GM had allegedly known about since 2008.[52]

Toyota's issue concerned "sticking" accelerators, which occurred between 2009 and 2010. The first recall pertained to a floor mat that could jam the gas pedal; the second, more serious, issue arose when the accelerator did not return to zero when released. Toyota recalled 9 million vehicles worldwide. Almost immediately thereafter, Toyota also issued a recall for a problem with its cars' antilock brakes. Given the scope of the recall, Toyota received some plaudits; however, eighty-nine people died.[53]

BP

A few years after the 1989 *Exxon Valdez* oil spill, Professor Fort's MBA ethics class at the University of Michigan discovered that, minutes after discussing the case, Exxon recruiters were setting up in the next room for a recruiting session. Several students challenged Exxon for its lack of responsiveness and preparedness for the spill. Exxon's response? "You are lucky it was us!"

As alarming—and remarkably frustrating—as that response was, perhaps Exxon had knowledge of how much worse it could have been. If the response was a prediction, it came true twenty-one years later in the BP Deepwater Horizon oil disaster. For nearly three months after an explosion destroyed the Deepwater Horizon oil rig, oil gushed into the Gulf of Mexico. Eleven people vanished and were never found. The spill is the largest of its kind in the petroleum industry, and the toxic impact on the environment was unprecedented. The spill also had an enormous effect on both personal health and economic interests, especially with respect to tourist beaches, fishing, and marine-based work.

Given the magnitude of the spill and contemporary sensitivities over the environment, it is not surprising that there was a significant national and international reaction to the daily images of the slick, the fire, and the consequences of the pollution. Yet, the public reacted perhaps even more negatively to the management of the disaster by BP. CEO Tony Hayward initially downplayed the incident as being "tiny" as compared with the magnitude of the entire ocean. Complaining about the amount of time he spent addressing the issue and the amount of criticism he faced, he said that he would like to have his life back, a comment that enraged those whose lives had been dramatically altered by the disaster.[54]

According to BP's own report, blame was shared by BP, Halliburton, and Transocean, which owned the rig. Both Halliburton and Transocean put the blame squarely on BP. Saying that there was not a culture of safety, the Oil Spill Commission found that there had been a "rush to completion" in constructing the rig, as well as shortcuts in management, such as using seawater rather than drilling fluid; the drilling fluid would have been heavy enough to prevent the methane gas from rising up the pipe and into the rig, which caused the explosion. The National Commission on the BP Deepwater Horizon Oil Spill and Offshore Drilling also cited shortcuts and poor management decision making in the operation of the rig.[55]

Hundreds of lawsuits were filed against BP, both in civil and criminal court. Those suits themselves became the subject of fraud charges, as BP claimed that many false or fraudulent claims were being filed. In 2015, BP estimated that the ultimate cost to BP of the spill was $18.7 billion.[56]

Factors and the Scandals

Not surprisingly, no (admirable) factor identified as most important by the executives seems to be present in these scandals. This suggests that these CEOs, at least, have a sense of what factors are important and, by implication, what happens when they are not present.

Table 3.3 captures each of the eight major factors identified by the CEOs and identifies the ways in which the companies in question failed to live up to them.

Table 3.3. Most important factors as applied to each of the corporate scandals.

	Tone at top	Standing behind values	Long-term orientation	Clear, well-understood policies	Listening to all stakeholders	Matching employee rewards and rhetoric	Leadership articulating importance of values	Continuous betterment of the company
Enron	Poor	Not at all	All short-term rather than long-term	On paper, perhaps, but no follow-through; not even cash flow and balance sheets	On paper, an attractive ethics and CSR program, but no evidence leaders cared at all about stakeholders	Not in terms of rhetoric of public statements, but yes in terms of encouraging "innovation" (whether legal or not)	No evidence for this	No evidence for this
Martha Stewart	Poor. Claimed to be victim more than addressing situation; also poor tone of conducting illegal trading	No evidence of this in terms of the insider trading dimension	Insider trading notoriously a short-term decision	Not applicable here given the divergence between personal trading decision and company policies	Public statement did suggest concern for employees and investors in the company; too little too late	Given the nature of this issue, the scandal wasn't in forcing employees to do something they might not do otherwise but instead was about how a leader's actions affect a company more broadly	Undermined her own statements through actions, though her statements to employees themselves may have articulated important values	Perhaps so with respect to employees
Lehman Brothers	Poor. All very short-term, manipulative, and illegal	Not at all	Not at all; all short-term	On paper, perhaps, but no follow-through	As with Enron, right statements made, but no evidence that these were pursued by the leaders	Same as Enron; not in terms of public statements	No evidence for this	No evidence for this

Ford/Firestone	Some at Ford; little at Firestone	Some at Ford, especially with its staffing of 1,000 people to help with customers; Little at Firestone given the deemphasis on quality and labor issues	In theory, both had long-term orientation given their history, but ample evidence of shortcuts, especially at Firestone	Ford much better at policies aimed at customers	Ford much better at listening to stakeholders, especially customers; problem for Firestone	Seems missing at Firestone given working conditions in Decatur plant; Ford less clear	Each company could have done better; Firestone in particular	Little evidence with Firestone; better evidence with Ford
GM/Toyota	Missing at GM; lacking at Toyota	Not well done at GM; Toyota more responsive on recalls in terms of protecting quality, but then the quality issues should have not arisen as dramatically in first place	Poor with GM; seems very short-term oriented, including decisions not to fix cars; Toyota seems too focused on short-term recovery from recession	Policies seem to encourage hiding problems, especially at GM	GM seemed to ignore stakeholders for a long time; Toyota more responsive, but at the beginning still more reactive and defensive than listening	GM certainly did not want to advertise its shortcutting; neither did Toyota, and so its rewarding for short-term solutions would fail to match employee rewards and company rhetoric	Missing at GM; some responsiveness with Toyota	Missing at GM; some acknowledgment at Toyota
BP	Lacking with complaints of CEO "to get his life back" pilloried in media	Company's vaunted environmental profile (Beyond Petroleum) significantly damaged	Intra-industry criticism of the quality of offshore oil drilling process	Lack of clarity as to how to respond to a sea-based oil spill; confusion as to next steps	BP did launch a huge PR effort and did solicit input; many have criticized the quality of engagement and empathy with stakeholders	Incentives for safety in drilling and in oversight on rig struggled to coincide with demands for maximum production and profitability	Rhetoric articulating values less of an issue than the institutionalization of those values and waffling at the time of the crisis	

Table 3.4. Virtues applied to problematic cases.

	Honesty	Integrity	Accountability	Sincerity	Loyalty	Resilience
Enron	A great deal of dishonesty	Definite integrity issues	No	No	Only among those conspiring to perpetrate the crimes	Perhaps so. Even among the miscreants, likely some degree of resilience to keep going through the scandal
Martha Stewart	Questions posed about dishonesty	With respect to trading, no, but company itself did not seem to necessarily lack this	Insider trading meant to avoid accountability; things do seem different with respect to company	Not individually; perhaps corporately	At least not at first, though later statements do try to address harmed employees and investors	Same as Enron
Lehman Brothers	A great deal of dishonesty	Definite integrity issues	No	No	Only among those conspiring to perpetrate the crimes	Same as Enron
Ford/ Firestone	Questions posed about dishonesty	Definite integrity issues with Firestone; less so from Ford, though still some problems	Both had major problems with accountability issues, especially Firestone	Both had issues in being forthcoming with public	Between the two of them, a century of loyalty shredded through actions	Same as Enron
GM/ Toyota	Questions posed about dishonesty from GM; less so from Toyota	Definite integrity issues	Both had issues with accountability, especially GM	Both had issues with being sincere, especially GM	Only among those conspiring to perpetrate the actions	Same as Enron
BP	Some questions posed about dishonesty, though ethical issues here were more associated with environmental rather than with	Definite integrity issues	Had issues with accountability in trying to throw off blame	Major sincerity issues, especially with respect to leadership	Only among those conspiring to perpetrate the actions	Same as Enron

THE NORM(S), LEADERSHIP, AND THE SCANDALS

Similarly, the participants in the corporate scandals largely lack the most important virtues identified by the CEOs: honesty, integrity, accountability, sincerity, loyalty, and resilience. There are more exceptions here because some of these virtues, such as loyalty and resilience, could well have been present as a feature of the relationships between the conspirators engaged in the misconduct. At the same time, these tend to be fairly minor exceptions compared to the entirety of the application of the virtues to the key scandals. (See Table 3.4.)

Of course, other factors pressured the participants in these situations to conduct themselves poorly. The pressure for demonstrating a strong return on investment certainly explains some of the shortcuts adopted by Enron, Lehman, and others. The desire to avoid a stock loss (outside of her own company's stock) was a strong motivator for Stewart.

4   Inspirational Stories of Integrity and Trust

If the paradigmatic case of a scandal is Enron, Johnson & Johnson's Tylenol case could be seen as its antithesis. It is so widely heralded as a case of exemplary behavior that it almost has become problematic. A cynic might ask, "Hasn't any company done something outstandingly good since 1982? If not, then isn't Johnson & Johnson simply the exception to the rule that business is systemically bad?" That argument has even more force considering J&J's own legal and ethical problems in the past ten years. During that time, it has been subject not only to governmental investigations but also to shareholders' derivative suits for failing to adhere to its long-standing culture.[1]

Yet the CEOs we interviewed reflected on the 1982 Tylenol case as one that "enhanced J & J's reputation, and more importantly the trust that consumers placed in their products." At least in hindsight, one of the more compelling arguments regarding the case is how hard it is to criticize. That is not because it has become iconic and therefore immune from negative comments. Instead, it is because it was a genuinely well-handled case, backed by people acting for all the right reasons. At the time, however, it was not so clear whether J&J was making a good business decision.

To briefly reprise the case, in 1982, seven people in the Chicago area mysteriously died.[2] Investigators quickly tied the deaths to each of the victims' ingestion of Extra Strength Tylenol that had been laced with cyanide. Although one person attempted to claim credit for the killings and demanded US$1 million to stop them, the murders have never been solved.[3]

As the link to Tylenol became known, many asked if there was a serious problem in Tylenol's manufacturing processes. This obviously concerned Johnson & Johnson, and, although there was no established link, the company had removed all bottles of the product from the shelves nation-wide within the week. In hindsight, this move has been widely praised as the key to J&J's rebuilding of trust with its customers and wider society. At the time, however, many questioned this decision. Did it amount to an admission of guilt? Would this trigger more and larger lawsuits? If the company did nothing wrong, why did it act as if it did?

Answering these questions and revealing the motivation for the action, CEO James Burke later explained that the company decided to remove all Tylenol from the shelves because, if it acted otherwise, the company could not live up to its Credo, which begins with an embrace of the re-sponsibility to provide safe products to all its customers.[4] Because leaving Tylenol on the market contradicted this aim, the company felt that it had to remove the product from the market.

The Credo, which was adopted when Johnson & Johnson made their public offering in 1944, includes a set of aspirations. Although the vi-brancy of the Credo may have diminished in the last decade or so, at the time of the Tylenol crisis, there is considerable evidence that the Credo played a strong role in J&J's culture. The company incorporated it into employee training as well as promotion and compensation decisions and held contests for the best story about the Credo in daily work each year. With a commitment to fair treatment of its stakeholders, especially its cus-tomers, CEO Burke's decision does not seem as extraordinary as it might seem otherwise. This statement, of course, is not a criticism; it is the op-posite. It is a recognition that the company was committed to an ethical course of action, and so ethical decisions resulted as a matter of course.

In the last chapter, we looked at the factors that the CEOs we surveyed believe to be most important in creating ethical business conduct. We also saw that very few, if any, of these factors were present in the companies at the heart of the scandals discussed in the previous chapter. How does J&J, at the time of the Tylenol crisis, fare based on the same criteria?

TONE AT THE TOP

CEO Burke's commitment to making the Tylenol decision on the basis of the Corporate Credo established a very clear tone at the top of what was important for the company.

STANDING BEHIND VALUES EVEN WHEN COSTLY

If there *ever* was a case of a company standing behind its values even when it appeared that it might be costly, the Tylenol decision is one of the best examples of this.

CLEAR, WELL-UNDERSTOOD POLICIES

The J&J Credo established a clear policy of commitments the company had, starting with a commitment to provide safe and effective products to doctors and to the customers who purchased them. This first commitment of the Credo was exactly the policy statement that was enacted.

LISTENING TO STAKEHOLDERS

This was done both implicitly and explicitly. Implicitly the aforementioned commitment to customers—a key stakeholder group—drove J&J to make the decision. In addition, it engaged in ongoing communication with various internal and external stakeholders to keep them apprised of the situation. This included changing the packaging of the product in the future to make it tamper proof.

MATCHING EMPLOYEE REWARDS AND RHETORIC

This seems less obvious from the dilemma per se, but, given the cultural expectation of rewards for following the Credo, this practice would make it easier—indeed expected—for any manager or executive to make the same decisions that CEO Burke and the board made.

LEADERSHIP ARTICULATING THE IMPORTANCE OF VALUES

This can be demonstrated through all the aforementioned factors.

CONTINUOUS IMPROVEMENT

This factor seems harder to pinpoint given the specificity of the dilemma itself.

In short, whereas the companies in the previous chapter's scandals failed just about each and every one of these factors, J&J passed just about each and every one with flying colors. There was another set of criteria we also examined in the previous chapter: the important virtues identified by the CEOs. Here again, J&J was exemplary, especially when compared to the negative examples in the previous chapter.

HONESTY

Rather than hiding information or deflecting blame onto others, J&J forthrightly shared the information it had available.

INTEGRITY

Not only was it honest, J&J also was holistically ethical because it dealt with the problem directly, even though there was no solid evidence that the company itself had done anything wrong.

ACCOUNTABILITY

Based on the preceding discussion, J&J made itself accountable for solving an issue that went beyond being accountable for a problem it created . . . but it did not create the problem (which is a more typical version of accountability). This is a proactive, beyond-the-rules version of accountability.

SINCERITY

J&J took the action it did because it sincerely believed in the Corporate Credo. That set everything else into motion.

LOYALTY

Whereas some of the cases in the previous chapter demonstrated loyalty only among coconspirators, in this case Johnson and Johnson exhibited loyalty to a much more important and broader range of stakeholders.

RESILIENCE

As previously noted, J&J's decision was, in hindsight, a brilliant defense of its brand. However, that was not so clear at the time its leaders made the decision. Instead, they relied on a sincere commitment to the aspirations of the Credo and banked on the resilience of the company to withstand the difficulties such an approach might create.

Because this chapter focuses on the positive rather than the negative affirmations of company actions, we want to follow the same approach as in the previous chapter and detail examples provided by the CEOs as to nominations for companies that engaged in exemplary behavior. Those companies (one of which is a government entity) are

1. Johnson & Johnson
2. Mattel
3. Maersk Shipping
4. Starbucks
5. Blue Bell Ice Cream
6. The city of Copenhagen
7. Costco
8. Arla

Examples of Good Corporation Actions

In addition to J&J, our CEOs named seven other companies as moral exemplars. Because the cases are relatively recent, there remain some judgments to be made as to how these actions will ultimately be viewed.[5] After all, as we have just noted, there were questions about J&J's handling of Tylenol early on. As we will explain, there seem to be trade-offs in many of these cases as well. As a result, they may not seem to be quite as noble as the Tylenol decision; however, it does not mean that there is not a strong example to learn from.

MATTEL

In 2007, Mattel Toys shocked the markets by issuing two product recalls. It recalled almost 500,000 toy cars depicting the jeep "Sarge" from the children's movie of the same name because the toys were contaminated with lead paint. The company also recalled 18.2 million other toys because they contained small magnets that posed choking dangers to children who might swallow them as well as potential internal injuries once ingested. All of the products had been manufactured in China.[6] The recalls followed hard on the heels of another set of problems with Mattel toys announced just a few weeks earlier. In these cases, lead paint was discovered in Barbie dolls, Hot Wheels cars, and toys featuring Sesame Street, Dora the Explorer, and Thomas the Tank Engine. In the previous year, problems with magnets had been found in Polly Pocket dolls and accessories.[7]

Mattel was founded in 1945 in a California garage. Harold Matson and Eliot Handler created and sold picture frames and then moved onto items such as Barbie and Hot Wheels. In 1960, the company made its public offering and continued to grow through acquisitions such as Fisher-Price and Tyco Toys. By 2002, as it grew and became more global, the company outsourced all of its production. By 2007, the company had issued fifteen product recalls.[8]

Mattel CEO Bob Eckert stated that, in investigating its earlier recall, the company found the additional problems that led it to voluntarily issue the second recall.[9] Bryan Stockton, executive vice president of Mattel International, said that the company's long-time Chinese subcontractor had failed to use certified paint on the products in question.[10] The company ran a full-page ad in *The New York Times*, and Eckert attended morning and evening news programs to apologize for Mattel's failure and promised solutions for quality issues. The company also launched a recall website. Many communications experts praised the company for its handling of the crisis.[11]

Indeed, the company had a long-standing reputation of being scrupulous with its safety and quality controls. A report on that exact issue—"Toy Making in China, Mattel's Way"—was released just a few days before the second recall.[12] After the recalls, New York University Professor S. Prakash Sethi raised concerns about what else might be occurring in the toy industry when he said, "If Mattel, with all of its emphasis on quality and testing, found such a widespread problem, what do you think is happening in the rest of the toy industry, in the apparel industry, and even in the low-end electronics industry?"[13]

A common reaction to this crisis was to blame Chinese manufacturers for using uncertified paint. This concerned Mattel as well, and it sought to own more manufacturing plants to better control production. The concern was not without cause. According to a *New York Times* article, every single toy that was recalled in 2007 had been manufactured in China, and the U.S. Consumer Product Safety Commission had doubled the amount of Chinese products recalled between 2002 and 2007.[14] Other prevalent safety concerns revolved around pet foods, pharmaceuticals, and toothpaste.[15]

Although lead-based paint on toys remained a concern in many of these recalls, at the center of the Mattel case was the presence of small magnets in the toys that could be swallowed by a child. Once in the body, the magnets could attract to one another and cause life-threatening internal injuries.[16] Reacting quickly, Mattel issued a product recall and focused its attention on Lee Der Industrial, the Chinese manufacturer responsible for painting the recalled toys. Shortly after the recall, Zhang Shuhong, Lee Der's owner, committed suicide, which further escalated the tensions surrounding the issue.[17]

Making matters worse, further investigation showed that the problem with the magnets was the result of a Mattel design flaw (through its subsidiary Fisher-Price) rather than negligence that occurred within the Chinese plant. Mattel apologized for targeting some goods as problematic that did, in fact, meet quality standards. Many toys had been recalled, Mattel explained, in an effort to ensure that its safety net was cast wide. The company noted that much of the problem had been created by Mattel's own designs rather than the paint itself.[18]

The Mattel recall bears significant resemblance to the Tylenol recall. Both companies were widely admired for their business approaches prior to the crisis each experienced. When the crises hit, both were responsive in the press, apologizing for problems, taking responsibility, and promising to get things right. Each launched recalls. In Mattel's' case, its hand was forced to some degree by regulatory pressure (and later the company did have to pay a US$2.3 million fine to the Consumer Product Safety Commission[19]), but a significant portion of the recalls in question were self-reported by Mattel. Both companies also revisited their manufacturing practices to ensure that any health and safety issues were addressed.

One key difference is that, by all reports, it seems that J&J was more of a victim, subjected to a third-party administering poison in its product, whereas Mattel's issues were the result of its own design issues and failure to oversee its own contractors. Yet this is not a definitive statement because the J&J case has never been closed. Mattel's actions won the praise of our CEOs for responsively and responsibly addressing a crisis.

MAERSK

As a global shipping giant, Maersk Shipping must frequently face difficult dilemmas that most of us are not experienced with. In 2009, Maersk was at the heart of what became an international situation (and later made into a film) when pirates boarded *MV Maersk Alabama* and took Captain Richard Phillips and his crew hostage off the coast of Somalia. Four pirates had boarded the ship, but Captain Phillips had altered radio frequency, disabled the navigation system, and broken the ship's phone so the pirates could not call for backup from their partners in crime. Marooned—so to speak—the pirates asked for a lifeboat and for Phillips to show them how to operate it, with the promise that he could return to the ship thereafter. Of course, once they were all on the lifeboat, they took Phillips hostage. Thereafter ensued the drama of Phillips's attempted escape and sharpshooters from the U.S. Navy Seals (*Alabama* was flying under the U.S. flag at the time and therefore open to U.S. military engagement), ultimately resulting in the deaths of the pirates and the sensational rescue of Phillips.[20]

Environmental issues may not provide the acute drama of pirates, Navy Seals, and hostages at sea, but during the same year Maersk also confronted a larger issue and dealt with it in a way lauded by our executives. In 2009, a series of articles documented that the Danish shipping conglomerate Maersk was responsible for as much pollution as the rest of the country of Denmark combined. Former CEO Nils S. Andersen promptly gave an interview with *Berlingske* newspaper, where he said that it was important to realize that "you are part of the problem," a candid acknowledgment so embraced by the company that it was reprinted in an official company publication.[21]

Jolted by the remarkable candor from its leader, Maersk executives decided to go beyond the curve of sustainability and stated that Maersk Shipping would reduce its carbon dioxide emissions by 20 percent per container by 2020. It would then increase its goal to 40 percent and then 60 percent. Former CEO Andersen said that at the time the company made the commitment, he had no idea how the company was going to achieve this goal but that it turned out to be a business advantage for the company.[22]

The company views this as a corporate social responsibility (CSR) approach, but not in a philanthropic sense. Instead, the company sought to turn CSR into a distinct competitive advantage. How does Maersk, or any company, transfer this noble goal into a profitable achievement? In this respect, Andersen's comments shed a bright light on a paradox of corporate responsibility. Andersen argued that the company does

> not do something simply because of sustainability. The aim is therefore to try to find ways in which to combine sustainability with business-improvement strategies. A cynic would say that my aim is to save fuel to make us more profitable. However, I would prefer my employees to get up every morning because they want to be part of creating a better world with reduced fuel

consumption and lower CO_2 emissions instead of them getting up and thinking how do I create a bit more, or a lot more, profit for the shareholders?[23]

This is one of the best cases we can present to lay bare the paradox of corporate responsibility. As a CEO, Andersen had to address shareholder profit. He was using CSR as an advantage insofar as one of the goals of CSR—in this case sustainability—is an independent good, worthy in its own right, even aside from shareholder profit. It is this wholehearted commitment to an independently worthy good that makes the likelihood of profit all the greater. Andersen wanted his employees to seek this good—to feel better about themselves and the company—and because of that independent good, the company's instrumental value increases. In other words, *the sincere pursuit of a non-economic good may be the most competitive economic strategy for business success.*

Andersen was quite specific about this advantage, claiming that the pride employees feel motivates them to give an additional "2 percent" because the company addresses a positive "extra." As another example, he mentioned a company biologist who was proud of the reclamation efforts Maersk made to restore a polluted waste dump. After the company's work was completed, fish returned to the port, and thousands of new jobs were created.[24]

Maersk claims that "strategic CSR" extends to other areas as well, such as contributing to the fight against Ebola by insisting on keeping its ports in Monrovia open at the time. The company also donated extra shipping resources in the aftermath of the devastating earthquake and tsunami in Japan in 2011.[25] Again touting the benefits to the approach, former CEO Andersen emphasized the importance of the company's name, ensuring it will be around for the next 100 years at least, with proud and motivated employees and bottom-line benefits.[26]

STARBUCKS

As with Maersk, Starbucks faces many issues pertaining to corporate responsibility, and the company uses this as a core business strategy. Although the employee turnover rate throughout the industry in 2000 was 220 percent, Starbucks boasted a 60 percent turnover rate, along with a survey showing that 82 percent of its employees (often called "partners" within the company) were very satisfied with their jobs.[27] The company also appeared in *Business Ethics Magazine* as one of its 100 "Best Corporate Citizens" the same year and also made the Top 100 of the "Best Global Brands" listed by *Business Week*.[28]

With such a reputation, the company was a natural target for Global Exchange, a nongovernmental organization (NGO) advocating for "fair trade" coffee.[29] Global Exchange demanded that Starbucks carry fair trade coffee in all of its cafes. Fair trade coffee is certified by Transfair USA, which imposes minimum price standards from producers that are democratically controlled by its members; importers are to purchase the coffee directly from the producers and establish long-term relationships with them and provide preharvest credits for each other; producers must implement crop management and environmental protection measures.[30]

Starbucks refused to switch suppliers, for fear of obtaining a lesser-quality bean; it did agree to create long-term agreements with its suppliers and to buy directly from suppliers whenever possible.[31] This would help farmers and suppliers to rise above poverty, maintain a high-quality product, and set an example for other companies. Starbucks' program is known as the Coffee and Farmer Equity (CAFÉ) program. In 2015, the company received a 99 percent ethical sourcing score.[32]

Starbucks also faced environmental challenges. It has been challenged on its contribution to deforestation caused by the production of palm oil. Palm oil is a common ingredient in consumer goods, as well as an alternative energy source. Finding palm for such uses has become a leading cause of deforestation in countries such as Malaysia and Indonesia. Not only does deforestation have an impact on wildlife; rain forests also absorb carbon dioxide. Given its history, Starbucks has been challenged to use only certified palm oil sources, a commitment that the company has made, though some critics argue it has been slow to implement its pledge.[33]

These social engagement initiatives aside, Starbucks also faced a deep internal issue. Becoming an iconic brand in the 1990s, the company faltered after the turn of the century. In 2008, the CEO who had led the company's growth in the 1990s, Howard Schultz, resumed the reins. Schultz's mantra was to maintain a small-company feeling while at the same time expanding the company, a topic to which we will return in Chapter 6.

To do this, Schultz investigated current store operations and found that quality had slipped in several ways. For example, in an effort to cut costs, baristas would steam milk for espresso and then reheat just before making a coffee for a particular customer. Stores were also making popular breakfast sandwiches, but Schultz believed that the smell of burning cheese undermined the "integrity" of the coffee romance and the aroma of coffee.[34]

This focus on quality and the emotional/sensory attributes of intimacy were crucial to Schultz's vision of keeping an intimate atmosphere while at the same time growing the company. He compared his vision to an English pub, where the coffee shop would be "a third space between home and work."[35] His vision was to make Starbucks "inspire the human spirit through values such as respect and dignity, passion and laughter, compassion, community, responsibility, and authenticity."[36]

To drive home the importance of these factors, Schultz took the dramatic step of closing all 7,100 stores in February 2008 to provide training to all 135,000 employees. His aim was to return to the finer things—like how to pour a "perfect" cup of espresso.[37]

In addition to this customer focus on quality and intimacy, the company remains committed to providing health insurance and college tuition assistance for all its employees and has an extensive CSR program of its own.

ARLA

In 2008 Arla's Chinese partner Mengniu Dairy was involved in a scandal concerning tainted baby milk powder in China. Other companies were also involved; according to the Chinese authorities. The milk powder was tainted with melamine, which is a chemical typically used in laminates, coatings, and plastics.[38] In small quantities, melamine poses no danger to humans, but it can pose serious risks to babies. A large number of Chinese dairies purchased the milk powder, including Arla Mengniu, which is a US$7.6 billion joint venture between a Chinese dairy and the venerable Danish company, Arla, to produce milk powder.[39]

The issue first came to light in September 2008 when the *Shanghai Daily* newspaper reported that fourteen infants had died in Gansu Province from drinking infant milk formula that was mixed with melamine.[40] The demand for milk in China had increased dramatically, growing from 1 million tons in 1995 to 18 million tons in 2006. Chinese dairy farmers, under pressure to keep prices low, first watered down the milk before selling it to larger dairy processing companies. To compensate for the resulting low protein content, melamine was then added to fool protein tests so it appeared that the milk contained more protein than it actually did.[41]

Ten days after the initial news of the milk crisis broke, Arla Mengniu detected melamine in its milk powder and liquid milk products.[42] The company recalled its entire product line immediately and halted production of all the joint venture's products until the reason for the contamination was determined; it also removed all its current products from retailers' shelves.[43]

The company's investigation confirmed that the contamination occurred at milk collection centers and not within Arla Mengniu's facilities, but the company apologized for the chemical's presence in their products anyway.[44] Over the next month, the company spent US$12.6 million on new melamine testing equipment and employed 8,000 employees to monitor contracted milk collection centers.[45] The company's products are now tested four times during production for melamine; in October 2008, the company restarted production, distribution, and sales of its products.[46]

BLUE BELL ICE CREAM

Making ice cream for over a hundred years, Blue Bell enjoyed an excellent reputation for safety and quality throughout its history. Indeed, through the first 108 years of its history, it never recalled a product for safety reasons. That history is one of the aspects of its 2015 controversy that makes its actions so difficult to analyze. A 108-year track record of safety counts for something; at the same time, what happened in 2015 caused many a skeptical eye to be cast on the ice cream maker's actions.

The company was founded in 1907 in Brenham, Texas, where it still has its corporate headquarters. Once focusing on selling both butter and ice cream, it has focused solely on the latter since the mid-1900s and now produces over 250 frozen novelties and ice creams, yogurts, and sherbets.[47] The Kruse family has owned the company since 1919, and their company employs about 3,000 people.

In 2015, three people died after consuming milk shakes made with the company's ice cream. Investigators discovered that the ice cream contained the listeria bacterium. Although the listeria did not cause the individuals' deaths per se, the deadly bacteria were a contributing cause.[48] The ice cream is so popular, especially in southern regions of the United States, that once the product was removed from the market, a black market developed for people desperate for the ice cream.[49]

The company was forced to recall some of its ice cream, as already noted, its first recall in its 108-year history. Blue Bell first shut down the facilities where the listeria was found and recalled the products produced there. Then it issued a second recall after reports of additional problems. Finally, the company voluntarily expanded the recall to its entire product line when it found problems in several of its manufacturing facilities.[50] It also enhanced its sampling program, which revealed more potential issues. Blue Bell, working together with governmental authorities, issued new safety measures that included more extensive cleaning and sanitizing, increasing testing of facilities by 800 percent, and sending daily samples to labs for more testing.[51]

The reaction to the recall has been decidedly mixed. On the one hand, the company did issue multiple voluntary recalls and, again staying a step ahead of governmental requirements, added additional testing that revealed more problems, which the company also addressed. One could argue that had the company not proactively undertaken these actions, more people would have become ill. This narrative seems to be consistent with a 108-year pristine history of providing safe products to the public. These efforts gained attention in our survey of CEOs.

Yet, there is a less rosy interpretation as well. Many media outlets and individuals were highly critical of the company's failure to maintain adequate health and safety oversight, which in turn led to contaminating factors, a fact made especially egregious when such missteps contributed to deaths.[52] In addition, evidence suggests that the company may have known of the contamination for several years, yet continued to sell its ice cream.[53] Further, the argument is that the company may have acted quickly, but that is also because it knew that if it did not, the government would force its hand.

At the current writing of this book, the evidence, to us, seems mixed as to how well Blue Bell carried out its response, even though their actions clearly caught the attention of our CEOs. Much of our assessment turns on the sincerity of the company's actions. If the company had known of this problem for several years and had done nothing, then it seems amiss to call their actions exemplary. The same holds true if it can be shown that the company was simply reacting to potential government action. On the other hand, if the evidence shows that the company was reacting as quickly as possible to a new situation and doing so regardless of potential government action, then the recall effort and the actions to sterilize the factories does impress. At this juncture, we believe that not enough evidence is in to fully assess the event.

CITY OF COPENHAGEN COUNCIL

Although our attention in this book is focused on for-profit businesses, our CEO survey nominated the city of Copenhagen. The nomination stemmed from the city's dealings with Ryanair and its subsequent refusal to allow any of its 45,000 employees to use the company for air travel.

Ryanair was founded in 1985 and is an airline company based in the Republic of Ireland. It has grown quickly; by 2014, it was the largest European airline in terms of scheduled passengers carried.[54] According to a July 2015 article in *The Guardian*, the company maintains an aggressive posture in terms of employment practices. It has been the subject of significant controversy over the years ranging from pilot rules, staff pressure, and vacation time.[55] Perhaps such controversies primed the pump for what occurred with the city of Copenhagen, but, regardless of those previous issues, the particular touchstone was the company's policy of not negotiating with unions, claiming that its experience demonstrates that employees prefer to negotiate directly with the company.[56]

The mayor of the city of Copenhagen invoked the EU term *social dumping* to characterize Ryanair's practices. That term is defined as a situation where foreign service providers undercut local service providers through lower labor standards.[57] In response, the Ryanair website featured a Photoshopped picture of the mayor as Marie Antoinette saying "Let them eat cake" and "Let them pay higher fares."[58] The company also closed its base in Billund airport just before unions were to begin a boycott. The good action here was the willingness of the city to stand up to a major business to uphold the rights of employees, to support local service providers, and to adhere to EU practices protecting such constituents.

COSTCO

Jim Sinegal and Jeff Brotman founded Costco in 1983. Since then, it has grown to over 450 locations and produces approximately US$100 billion in annual revenue. Similar to Johnson & Johnson, the company was built on a commitment to a set of values; in order of priority, "to obey the law; take care of our members; take care of our employees; respect our suppliers; and reward you, our shareholders."[59]

Costco's employees receive an average wage of US$17 per hour, higher than those of its competitors, which tend to pay closer to minimum wage level of US$7.25; Costco also provides health and dental insurance; 401(k) plans; and paid vacation, holiday, and sick time for both full-time and part-time employees. The company has low turnover, low employee theft, high employee satisfaction, and low union participation.[60]

In 2004 and 2005, the company was criticized by some analysts as being too generous to employees.[61] Some analysts worried that the company was not sufficiently focused on efficiency and profitability in a very competitive market (including such competitors as Walmart and Sam's Club) and possibly "taking money away from shareholders and giving it to employees and customers." Sinegal responded admirably that

> On Wall Street, they're in the business of making money between now and next Thursday. . . . we can't take that view. We want to build a company that will still be here 50 and 60 years from now.[62]

Following on themes articulated by Maersk's CEO Anderson, Sinegal further rejected the notion that the company's approach was altruistic, arguing instead that it was simply good business.[63]

Costco's approach from a financial standpoint seems to have been a tremendous success, Wall Street sniping aside. Since its initial public offering in 1985, the company's stock has risen by nearly 900 percent, much higher than its competitors. Furthermore, in that same 2004–2005 period in which Costco faced its Wall Street detractors, Costco stock appreciated by 50 percent while Wal-Mart dropped by 10 percent.[64] (See Table 4.1.)

As one would expect, the factors the CEOs identified as being most important were overwhelmingly present in these "good" cases. In almost every case there was a strong "tone at the top," with senior leadership providing clear policies and a sense of the importance of the company's values, not only to the company but to a wider cause as well. In each case, the company and its leaders embraced a long-term commitment and often very explicitly rejected "short-termism." The companies were "in it" for long-term success, and that made a difference to their perception of the value of their reputation and how their actions would pay off in the long run. There was also a strong emphasis on the importance of listening to stakeholders to assist in providing solutions to the company's problems and, in particular, of the value of employees, rewarding them for the values the companies sought to embrace.

Thus, although we saw that these factors were mostly absent in the previous chapters' examples of companies that stumbled, often badly so, the exemplary cases highlighted in this chapter feature these factors. We have strong reason to believe that these factors provide crucial evidence of how companies can lead and perform ethically in a way that is simultaneously profitable.

THE NORM(S), LEADERSHIP, AND THE EXEMPLARS

These same considerations hold true for the norms the companies and their leaders practice. Virtues such as honesty, integrity, accountability, sincerity, loyalty, and resilience were as regularly featured in these exemplary stories as they were absent in the accounts from the previous chapter's recounting of corporate standards.

Although all of these virtues were present, one of the more interesting aspects of the CEOs' comments was the importance of pursuing a noneconomic goal for its own independent value. That was true of Maersk's sustainability and Johnson & Johnson's Credo as well as Mattel's commitment to safety, the council of the city of Copenhagen's and Costco's sense of fairness, and Starbuck's sense of quality and intimacy. Each of these companies pursue a "good" that each had identified because it was valuable apart from its economic aspect.

Here again, we see the importance of sincerity in pursuing these noneconomic "good" values, and, in sincerely pursuing them, the companies reach their highest economic value. When the "good" values lost their independent value—as in the case of Starbucks—trouble ensued until Schultz reinstituted this value.

Just as the previous chapter's examples showed few or none of the positive factors and none of the virtues identified by the CEOs, the examples of this chapter seem to reinforce each one of them. Of course, one might argue there is some circularity to this logic. The executives named the factors, the virtues, and the good and bad examples; so it follows that they know the examples are good or bad because of those same factors and virtues. How else can one know something is good or bad unless one has some kind of criteria—that is, the factors and virtues—that can be used to make such judgments? We assert that the values and factors identified by the executives will resonate with people as being intrinsically "good" values. One of Professor Fort's former doctoral students liked to say that

Table 4.1. Most important factors as applied to each of the corporate exemplars.

	Tone at top	Standing behind values	Long-term orientation	Clear, well-understood policies	Listening to all stakeholders	Matching employee rewards and rhetoric	Leadership articulating importance of values	Continuous betterment of the company
Johnson & Johnson	Very strong	The paradigmatic case	Core to company	Strong via Credo	Key to Credo and key to success	Evidence demonstrates real rewards for implementing Credo	Very strong and clear	Very strong
Mattel	Strong	Strong	Core to company	Clear and well known, though design defects did trip up manufacturers with respect to lead paint	Key to company's commitment to customers, children, and even to manufacturers when wrongly blamed	Less explicit evidence, but employees demanding quality seem to have been supported	Very strong and clear	Very strong
Maersk	Very strong	Making a problem into an advantage	Core to company	Explicit through goals for carbon dioxide reduction	Key to understanding the relationship between goods pursued for their own independent value and profitability	Less explicit evidence, but employees demanding CSR seem to have been supported	Very strong and clear	Very strong

Starbucks	Very strong	Dramatically righting the corporate ship	Core to company	Clear and well understood but needed reinforcement when sliding occurred	Key to reclaiming its customer base with the experience of quality and intimacy of coffee experience	Made very explicit to do exactly this when Schultz returned as CEO	Very strong and clear	Very strong
Blue Bell	Rhetorically strong, the depth of which is too early to tell	Perhaps; it turns on the sincerity of the reaction and actions	Depends on whether evidence was hidden previously; if so, then problematic; if not, then actions to clean up factories very good	If following long tradition of quality, then yes, but if evidence bears out of hiding problems, then that very act would undermine clarity	Assuming an authentic reaction to the problem, then very good; if revealing a hidden practice ignoring stakeholder safety, then not	Currently unclear	As with other aspects of this matrix, dependent on sincerity of actions to clean up a recently revealed problem	As with other aspects of this matrix, dependent on sincerity of actions to clean up a recently revealed problem
City of Copenhagen Council	Very strong	Very strong in refusing to work with Ryanair	Less explicit but seems implicit		As public entity, listening to stakeholders was key to the city's need to stand up to Rynnair	Less explicitly clear; need more information	Very strong articulation of values	Need more information
Costco	Very strong	Very strong	Core to company		Explicitly institutionalized in company strategy	Seems core to the company's operations	Very strong and clear	Very strong

Table 4.2. Virtues as applied to exemplary cases.

	Honesty	Integrity	Accountability	Sincerity	Loyalty	Resilience
Johnson & Johnson	Strong	Strong	Strong	Strong	Strong	Strong
Mattel	Strong	Strong	Strong	Strong	Strong	Strong
Maersk	Strong	Strong	Strong	Strong	Strong	Strong
Starbucks	Strong	Strong	Strong	Strong	Strong	Strong
Blue Bell	Strong	Perhaps strong; did it follow regulations?	Strong	Perhaps strong, but open question of whether proactive or reactive	Strong	Strong
Copenhagen	Strong	Strong	Strong	Strong	Strong	Strong
Costco	Strong	Strong	Strong	Strong	Strong	Strong
Arla	Strong	Strong	Strong	Strong	Strong	Strong

he never saw a company website that touted its corruption, insincerity, and criminal outlook. Instead, company websites tout the things the executives identified, which demonstrates that these virtues and factors are, indeed, good ones, and ones that can be used to evaluate company actions. If that is true, then we can use them to evaluate companies whose actions run afoul of such conduct and also to see those companies that make ethics work. They seem to do best when they value the ethical conduct as possessing its own independent "good."

Chapters 3 and 4 thus provide a baseline of what is good corporate conduct. In the following chapters, we analyze this further in terms of implementing decisions and creating ethical corporate cultures. In doing so, we rely on the executives' identification of positive factors and virtues. We also add a few additional ones to offer a way for "best practices" to become even better.

PART II

From Integrity and Trust to
Authenticity and Sincerity

5 Making Good Decisions about Strategy, Ethics, and Leadership

Hardheaded business leaders tend to scrupulously follow rigorous decision making when the topic pertains to marketing, strategy, or finance, but when it comes to issues pertaining to integrity, trust, and ethics the rigor is often lacking. Why is this? When asked why, many have replied with variations on the following: "Ethics is private and personal." "Either you have integrity, or you don't." "I'm a good person; I rely on my gut, and I make trustworthy choices."

There is reason to be concerned about this approach. Annual surveys show that up to 90 percent of us think that we are good, ethical people, and we consider that less than 50 percent of the rest of the population is.[1] Perhaps some, maybe even most of us give too much credit to how good we think we are. The reason is that we can rationalize whatever we do as being acceptable while demonizing what someone else does as being bad.

Consider, as an example, driving a car in a crowded metropolitan area. Within five minutes, you are likely to be cut off by another driver, or another driver will do something to greatly annoy you. When this happens, do you stop and reflect for a moment to try to figure out why the other person cut you off? Do you concern yourself with the possibility that the person might be driving to the hospital frantically because a family member has just been rushed there in an ambulance?

Probably not. More likely, your reaction is to slam your hand on the car horn and perhaps shake your fist, finger, or something else at the other driver while uttering a less than pleasant expletive at him. You might even say, "What kind of a person would drive like that?" When you do this, you are making a moral judgment about the person ("what kind of a person?") and likely thinking the worst about the other driver.

But what if you act in the same manner? What if you cut off another person for any of the possible reasons mentioned? When that other driver beeps her horn or shakes her fist, you may dismissively think, "Give me a break; I've got to get somewhere fast." You have rationalized why your behavior is justified. We give ourselves credit for having a good reason while not necessarily giving the same benefit of the doubt to someone else. That is why 90 percent of us think we are model citizens, whereas the rest of the population is comprised of people lacking integrity.

This kind of self-serving, rationalizing psychological bias holds real danger for making leadership decisions. The good decisions the CEOs recognized in our survey did not appear to be easy knee-jerk reactions. Instead, they followed considered approaches to decision making, especially in decisions that were consistent with the identity and history of the firm itself. Correcting for self-serving biases requires a rigorous and disciplined analysis of ethical choices.

Other excuses for why we do not undertake rigorous decision making in ethics holds true as well. The notion that ethics is personal and private does, of course, hold some truth. Our values define who we are as human beings, and so the ethical decisions we make are very personal. Yet they almost never can be wholly private for two reasons.

We tend to intervene when people make choices that harm other people. Making ethical decisions is *always* about how we treat others, so ethics can *never* be purely private. Others are always affected, and they (and others) will react to our choices.

It is true, of course, that there are circles of privacy. One would be hesitant to interfere with the choices a parent makes for his or her child or to intervene between spouses. There is some privacy accorded to such choices. But it is not absolute. Society does step in when there is abuse in the home, and so, even there, the choices people make are not purely personal and private.

Second, business leaders make ethical decisions on behalf of others in their leadership roles. So even if CEOs would like to keep ethics personal and private, the decisions they make in their role as CEO are not private. The choices may still have a strong personal dimension to them, but they are not private. The job of CEOs and board members is to lead, and the tone set and training provided become crucial for the employees who work in the company.

In an interview for a set of ethics classes at George Washington University, a leading corporate responsibility consultant, Ellen Mignoni of APCO Worldwide, stated:

> Some of the better practices that I've seen (especially recently over the last few years, I would say) is that, number one: there is a lot of clarity around what the company's policy procedures are and what their expectations are. They really do set a tone. That tone has to be set at the top, and it has to be driven across the business units inside an organization . . .
>
> The second piece is really, are we communicating that on a regular basis? Again, it is critically important to make sure that employees understand what those expectations are and that they talk about them so that they become really a part of who I am as an employee at this institution or at this organization . . .
>
> It's training . . . It's helping people work through and think through what could be real-life situations . . . and give them the skills, give them the resources that they need to address those in a way that the company is saying that they want them to be addressed. And then finally, I think it has to be part of an annual review—it has to be a part of an employee's evaluation.[2]

The final crutch is that one either has integrity or one does not. Yet we should think about how we make ethical decisions for three reasons.

First, there are some people who may simply be sociopaths. Ghandi once said that the law is not necessary for 5 percent of the population because they are going to be good regardless of what the law says; nor is it helpful for the 5 percent at the other end of the spectrum because they aren't going to care what the law says. The work, he said, was in the 90 percent of us who have some good ideas about behavior, have temptations too, and need nudges here and there to do what we know we should.[3] The danger, as we have already seen, is that any of us might tend to think of him- or herself as one of those top 5 percent when, in reality, we are more likely to be in that middle 90 percent. Although there may be some who have wholehearted integrity and some who are "lost causes," most of us are in the middle.

Second, the notion that "you either have integrity, or you do not" turns ethics into an attribute rather than a learnable skill. However, the evidence demonstrates that it is also a skill. Making ethical decisions, as Aristotle stated, can be hard work. It takes wisdom, skill, or what Aristotle called "phronesis," to make good decisions. Just as a violinist, quarterback, or executive becomes a good decision maker through practice, so too do we make better decisions by developing skills. That requires practice, education, and training.

Third, there is some evidence that suggests that much of our moral character is formed at a young age. However, there is also evidence that shows that we adapt to the societies and cultures in which we live throughout our lives. That is true as we adapt to cultures and behaviors in the workplace and beyond retirement.[4] Moreover, even if we have the character to say "be kind to others," that moral rule—learned in our early childhoods—does not necessarily tell us what to do when we are in the working environment. Decision making is not self-defining.

The reality is that we can make better decisions if we apply the same rigor to our ethical decision making as we do to other issues we confront. We need to do so if we are going to be able to garner trust and be viewed as having integrity ourselves. With this in mind, we propose an eight-step decision-making model. This model can be divided into three parts: (1) understanding and addressing our psychological biases; (2) applying key steps to reaching a decision; (3) carrying forward the steps to creating cultures that reinforce good decision making. The last of these three parts will be addressed in Chapter 7.

Psychological Biases

WHAT AND HOW WE SEE

Many of our moral disagreements arise from seeing things differently.[5] If two people cannot learn to describe what they see and are not able to understand what the other person is seeing, then the only thing that will change in their debate will be the decibel level.

Look at Figure 5.1. Is this a picture of a young woman or an old woman? The answer, of course, is that both are present. The young woman is looking away from the camera with her hair flowing down her back; she is wearing a necklace. The old woman looks to the side and down. What was an ear to the young woman is an eye to the old woman. What was a necklace becomes the lips of the old woman. What was the young woman's chin becomes the old woman's nose. If one adamantly focuses on one way of looking at the picture, it can be very difficult to step

Figure 5.1. Photo of old woman/young woman.
Source: William Ely Hill.

back and see it in a different light. A person who sees only one woman may be right to insist on what he or she sees, but this person may not see all of what is there.

Figure 5.2. An example of Rubin's vase.
Source: Edgar Rubin.

To take another example, does Figure 5.2 show a picture of a vase or of two people looking at each other? As with the "young woman/old woman" picture, the answer is both; it depends on how one looks at it.[6]

These illusions are amusing, but they have ethical implications as well. If you see an old lady and another person sees a young lady, your argument as to who is right will be futile. You become more frustrated in your disagreement unless one (or both) of you start to describe what he or she sees and then takes the time to try to see things from another's point of view. Thus, one step of ethics is simply learning to describe what we see—akin to values clarification—and then learning to articulate to others what we are seeing and stopping to listen to what the other person is seeing.

Two Vignettes on "Seeing"

As mentioned briefly at the beginning of the book, Lawrence Kohlberg wrote an interesting vignette, "The Story of Heinz,"[7] which demonstrates the difference of how we see things. This is how Kohlberg put it:

A woman was near death from cancer. One drug might save her, a form of radiation a pharmacist in the same town had recently discovered. The pharmacist was charging US$2,000.00, ten times what the drug cost to produce. The sick woman's husband, Heinz, approached everyone he knew to borrow the money, but he could only put together about half this amount. He told the pharmacist that his wife was dying and asked him to sell it cheaper or let him pay later. But the pharmacist refused. The husband got desperate and broke into the man's store to steal the drug for his wife.[8]

Did Heinz do the right thing? How does one know what is the right thing to do? Should Heinz have found an alternative method to get the drug? What would that have been? Was the pharmacist unethical? Should laws require a pharmacist to provide drugs in situations like these?

The Heinz case is a classic moral dilemma. There are at least two ways of seeing the issues in this case, and once one is focused just on one of them, it becomes hard to see the other side. Moreover, as mentioned at the beginning of this book, this exact situation has been replicated during the writing of this book, first with Turing Pharmaceutical's increasing of the HIV drug Daraprim 5,455 percent and then with price increases of the EpiPen. In the final analysis, it is difficult to support such extreme price increases for those in significant need of a medicine, especially when contrasted with Novo Nordisk's sale of insulin in Africa at a price level 20 percent of the market price in the affluent West. At the same time, within less extreme examples, there are pressures pulling in different directions on companies, not simply in terms of short-term versus long-term profits, though there is that, but also in terms of what the optimal societal results are as well.

Here is another example of seeing, from an actual legal case set in Florida:

The respondents, Ernest and Regina Twigg, have alleged that 10 years ago personnel at Hardee Memorial Hospital in Wauchula, switched their healthy newborn daughter with another girl born on approximately the same date to Robert Mays' late wife, Barbara, and that both couples went on to raise children not actually their own natural offspring. The child raised by the Twiggs, Arlena Beatrice, later died from a congenital heart condition. Shortly before Arlena's death the Twiggs learned, based on the child's blood type, that neither of them could have been her biological parent. Kimberly Mays was the only other white female in occupancy at Hardee Memorial Hospital at the time of Arlena's birth. The respondents began the underlying litigation by filing a

"Petition for Order Compelling Blood Test to Confirm Paternity of Female Child," later substituting a complaint for declaratory relief. The amended complaint demands a declaration that Kimberly Mays is the Twiggs' natural biological child.

Assuming that both the Twiggs and Mr. Mays are good parents, who should be permitted to parent Kimberly? How someone "sees" this case is crucial to deciding it. If the mental viewing frame is about "parental rights," then it is likely the decision will hinge on the perception that this is a case of deeply frustrated parental rights (the Twiggs).[9]

If one sees this case as one of rights associated with being a parent, then the Twiggs, who had their daughter taken from them through no fault of their own, should raise Kimberly. She is, officially, their daughter. But is seeing this through the lens of the rights of parents the best way to look at it? If someone "sees" the moral issue as focused on the best interests of the child, a different decision is possible. Doesn't parenting a child for ten years count for something as well? How does one resolve this case? How would one get each side to see the other's point of view? If this can be achieved—getting each side to see the other point of view—does that provide any additional possible ways to resolve the case?[10]

These "seeing" vignettes are part and parcel of what occurs in corporate life as well. In another of the interviews recorded for MBA classes at George Washington University, Dara Lubarsky, a young account executive for a corporate recruiting firm, explained how different stakeholders can "see" a situation very differently, with ethical judgments resulting directly from the perspective:

> My co-worker got his candidate through to the "offer" stage. At that point, the client requested that the background check be administered. It turns out the candidate didn't pass his background check.
>
> The client accused my co-worker of unethical representation of this candidate and falsely representing him. Yet, we never claim as part of our service that background check. That's always in the hands of the client at the end of the process.
>
> So, the client views it as us misleading (being unethical) in our representation, and we view it as, whose responsibility is this due diligence, really?[11]

These "vignettes" and pictures demonstrate the importance of being aware of how we see things and how others might see them as well. They provide a test for just how crucial it is for us to be aware of what we are seeing and to develop the capability of explaining what we see and experience, so that someone else knows what we are talking about. That is true of the pictures, of course, graphically; it is also true of our ethical ideas. And that description is even truer when there are so many stakeholders these days who do have a voice to critique what a company is doing. If a company intends to uphold its integrity, then it needs to be able to articulate what its vision is. There may still be disagreement, but some of that may well be muted if the basis of what we see is well articulated.

ADDITIONAL BIASES

Another part of moral psychology argues that human beings' innate biases often hamper our capability to make objective ethical choices.[12] Because we want to fit in, we tend to recast information we receive to justify being part of our desired group.[13] We tend to be overconfident in our own abilities and therefore downplay risks associated with our actions.[14] We value our own self-interest over the self-interest of others.[15] Once we cross the line of taking a questionable action, we can find ourselves heading down a slippery slope of decisions as our ethical norms fade into the background.[16] When we step into a role, we jettison the values we would typically rely on and adopt another set of values that could "justify" problematic behavior.[17] Many such ethical biases have been documented in business, all of which share the central characteristic of challenging the functioning of our moral conscience.[18]

Our biases also affect how we act in our role; how a slippery slope can lead us from one thing to another, one step into another; our predisposition to give ourselves permission to do something "bad" if we believe we have done something "good"; and how we jettison our independent judgment to fit into our reference group.

In short, there are many psychological biases that could distract us from making good, morally based decisions. Believing that our intuition will simply tell us what to do, or that we are good people who will make good choices, sets us up for self-deception, which could undermine our integrity and trustworthiness. Thus we need a matrix or process to keep ourselves honest with ourselves and true to the values of an organization and others.

Such a reminder/process/matrix helps employees make decisions. Sarah Schwarzbeck, a recent graduate working in an investment hedge fund, made this observation in an interview:

My company—we operate on a set of principles. These principles are written by our CEO, and there are a set of management principles—not to live by, necessarily, but to manage by. And they really embody three virtues: honesty, integrity, and excellence.

These are present in every single thing that we do—whether it be with our clients, or internally—we strive to achieve. And the principles in and of themselves are very much the backbone of what we do in our daily lives and with our teams.

I think that these principles are a constant reminder of what it means to be excellent. And having them as a reference is really something that is helpful during times of conflict or dispute, and that's something that I found personally to be helpful to me in operating ethically within my day-to-day.[19]

Schwarzbeck's example highlights the need for the articulation of specific commitments or benchmarks to use in making decisions. Those principles are, in her words, "constant reminders" of what people should consider in making decisions in business. They move individuals away from their innate biases by forcing attention toward solid principles of conduct. Similarly, a decision-making process helps any person to counter biases and to keep one honest with oneself, as well as to systematically make good decisions.

LaRue Tone Hosmer was one of the founders of the modern field of business ethics. A successful entrepreneur, Hosmer left his lumber business to obtain his doctorate from the Harvard Business School and then became a professor at the University of Michigan. After years of focusing on issues of entrepreneurship and strategy, he committed to the study of ethics, in part because his own business experience made him realize the challenges, temptations, and opportunities that exist in business life. Thus, unlike many professors of business ethics, Hosmer was an accredited businessperson who brought a grounded practicality to his work.

His six-step decision-making process is not revolutionary. Indeed, this is one of its strengths. It is not that ethical decision making is necessarily different than in marketing or strategy decision making but that we oddly think that ethics proceeds more intuitively than in these other fields. But, as we have already argued, this is not the case. Making good ethical decisions is as much of a skill as making good marketing or strategy decisions. It requires knowledge and analysis; intuition can be helpful, of course, but the essential skills do not differ.

We have added a step to Hosmer's process. Hosmer's work preceded the major work in the application of moral psychology to business decisions, although, given his own experience, he was keenly attuned to the problems of psychological bias. Indeed, the impetus for his six steps was to counteract such self-serving rationalizations.

DECISION-MAKING STEPS

If "step one" is to be aware of psychological biases, the next six steps of Hosmer's moral reasoning process are as follows:[20]

2. Identify the moral issue.

3. Identify additional facts helpful to making a decision.

4. Identify the alternatives available to apply to the problem.

5. Identify the personal impacts to the decision maker.

6. Apply the three leading contemporary theories of business ethics: shareholder, stakeholder, and virtue.

7. Conclude with a decision.

Consider, for example, the controversy surrounding the 2015 Volkswagen case.[21] The company possessed an exceptional brand identity, especially grounded in its success during the 1960s with its famous Beetle. As of 2015, it had produced three of the top-ten best-selling cars of all time.[22] In 2008, the company pioneered efforts to make a "clean" diesel car, one that combined high performance with environmental considerations.[23] This challenge proved to be much greater than Volkswagen anticipated, and the company struggled to find a way for its diesel cars to meet U.S. environmental standards. The dilemma culminated in a statement released by the Environmental Protection Agency, which, on September 18, 2015, laid out the problem in stark terms:

> Today, EPA is issuing a notice of violation (NOV) of the Clear Air Act (CAA) to Volkswagen AG, Audi AG and Volkswagen Group of America, Inc. (collectively referred to as Volkswagen). The NOV alleges that four-cylinder Volkswagen and Audi diesel cars from model years 2009–2015 include software that circumvents EPA emissions standards for certain air pollutants.[24]

It is one thing for a company to fail emissions standards. It is another to allegedly create a computer program that would systematically hide the failure. Tests showed that the cars were emitting forty times more than the EPA standards, which had implications for individuals with respiratory issues. Nearly 500,000 cars were recalled in the United States, and Volkswagen admitted that 11 million cars worldwide were similarly equipped.[25]

The company immediately owned up to the problem. The CEO and president of the company's North American division stated, "We've totally screwed up."[26] The cost to the company is estimated to be in the billions of dollars simply to cover the costs of the recalls.[27] A week after the scandal erupted, CEO Martin Winterkorn resigned and additional high-ranking executives were suspended.[28]

STEP TWO: IDENTIFY THE MORAL PROBLEM

A simple way of figuring out the moral issue is by looking at who is being "harmed." As an example, just because your favorite team loses a game, it does not create an ethical dilemma. Just because you lose a job, it does not mean you have created an ethical dilemma.

There will inevitably be winners and losers. Thus, in identifying a moral issue, one is looking at a situation where there has been harm inflicted, particularly to a vulnerable party, to someone who has been unable to protect him- or herself particularly well. To list some more serious situations, in the Mattel case, children consumed lead; in the Tylenol case, people ingested cyanide; in the Lehman Brothers and Enron cases, investors lost money while being misled to believe that these companies were in good shape. These raise certain ethical issues.

In the Volkswagen case, the most immediately apparent group that was harmed were those with respiratory problems exacerbated by the high levels of nitrogen released by the vehicles. Other environmental harms are that the chemical contributes to global warming and acid rain, and, of course, there is an issue of a possible violation of the law.

Or consider the BP Deepwater Horizon spill. There were countless vulnerable stakeholders who felt the direct impact of the disaster, beginning with those who lost their lives when the explosion occurred on the oil rig; to the residents of coastal areas whose livelihoods and homes were affected by the oil; to the wildlife, especially in the Gulf, literally swimming in contaminated fluids; to the shareholders whose investments were harmed from the cleaning costs and lawsuits that resulted.

STEP THREE: ADDITIONAL FACTS

Businesspeople tend to search for many additional facts before they make a decision. As one may often be required to make decisions based on insufficient information, it is an important attribute to identify additional facts necessary to make good moral decisions.

In the Volkswagen case, it would be interesting to know who knew about the software and at what levels this strategy became operational. Was this strategy adopted at the highest levels of the company, or was it designed "under the radar" of executive oversight? From a consequential point of view, it would be helpful to know exactly how many people have been harmed—or who may be harmed in the future given the environmental residue involved—to more fully determine appropriate accountability. What industry and shareholder pressure drove the motivation to create the flawed software strategy?

In the BP case, it would be helpful to know why safety precautions were not in place and why cleanup efforts were not better rehearsed in advance. Or consider the issues of Mylan, the maker of the EpiPen. Shortly after the news stories broke about the cost increases of the EpiPen, the company rushed a cheaper generic version of the product to the market. Was this something that had previously been planned or was it simply an effort to react to the bad publicity?

STEP FOUR: AVAILABLE ALTERNATIVES

Sometimes, we may think of an ethical issue as an "either/or" choice. "You must either do the saintly thing or risk selling your soul." Should GM, Ford, or Toyota recall all their cars? Or none of them? Or some of them? Should Firestone stop manufacturing all tires until it can figure out why they are exploding? Or do nothing? Are there steps in between these "either/or" situations?

In the Volkswagen case, prior to the exposure of the problem, one might ask if the company had other ways to achieve the combination of power and cleanliness, or whether this was this a flawed project from the start that should have been abandoned much earlier. Even though there would have been damages and costs to the company, these costs may have been substantially less than what the company must now confront.

Looking at the case after the scandal erupted, the company had the alternative to cease production of the vehicles or to announce a voluntary recall more quickly, or the company could have dug its heels in and challenged the governmental recall. Although not all these choices were likely to be successful, they do represent available alternatives.

Would it be possible for Turing or Mylan to remain profitable with a lower price for their products? Aren't there alternative ways to decide who should get the next World Cup without resorting to bribery for FIFA? Also pertaining to FIFA, but on a different issue, to prevent exploitation of human rights workers, could FIFA require—and monitor—standards for the practices of the countries and companies that build stadiums for the World Cup?

STEP FIVE: ASSESS PERSONAL IMPACTS

Assume that you are in the position of being the decision maker, or a person who is making a recommendation to the decision maker. What are the consequences to you personally, and what are the consequences to your career in the decisions you make? From a career standpoint, it can be viewed in many ways. If the company thinks, for example, that you are spending too much money, you may be viewed as a profligate spender, and therefore you risk being fired.

On the other hand, if you ignore the problem, you could become the scapegoat. The other party, whoever they are, would say, "You know, if Tim had told me there was a problem, I would have done something about it. He stayed quiet; he's to blame." Recognize that, as you are assessing a given situation, the personal impacts could have varied results.

Consider, for example, BP's Tony Hayward's lament that he "wanted his life back," as we noted at the beginning of the book. Although he was clearly feeling the personal impacts as he tried to lead BP's efforts to address the problem, his comments outraged a public who were demanding answers to the Deepwater Horizon disaster and its terrible impact on the environment.

As you make decisions, it is worth reflecting on how these decisions will affect you. Given the resignation of both the North American CEO of Volkswagen and the CEO of its parent company, the consequences are plain to see.

STEP SIX: APPLY THREE MORAL FRAMEWORKS

Shareholder Theory   Shareholder theory is the theory that is most frequently used in business schools today. Shareholder theory typically is thought of as the duty of a manager to maximize shareholder profitability. However, from a legal perspective, shareholder theory is that managers have a duty to carry out the lawful directives of the shareholders. One of those lawful directives is undoubtedly to make a profit. By necessity, companies must stay in business.

However, it is important to remember that there can be noneconomic lawful directives that managers are also required to pay attention to. Let us look at three different kinds of companies that could have a different sense of what shareholder theory looks like. For instance, in a family-held business or a closely held business where there may be ten to thirty shareholders, it is plausible that all the shareholders would decide on various noneconomic directives that they wish to pursue. They may decide that they will devote 10 to 15 percent of their profits to a local community charity or that they will focus on hiring people with specific capabilities. This is perfectly legal even though this exercise would undoubtedly cost more. Thus, with a small business there may exist the ability to define quite precisely those noneconomic objectives.

At the other end of the spectrum would be a large publicly held company with a million shareholders. The only common denominator among the shareholders' goals may be making a profit. In this situation things are more complicated, as there are many opinions that need to be taken into account.

The third type of company are those that were once family owned, and they let it be known at the time of their initial public offering that "if you want to invest in us, realize that we dictate the company's priorities." For instance, Johnson & Johnson has its famous Corporate Credo, which was first articulated in the 1940s at the time the company made its initial public offering. The Credo lists the stakeholders to whom the company has responsibilities. At the top of the list are doctors, nurses, and parents; next on the list are their employees, their suppliers, the community, and the government. And last, the Credo says if we have met the objectives for all these stakeholders, our shareholders will get a fair return on their investment. As a matter of property law, shareholders could overturn the Corporate Credo, but it does serve as a medium between investors, potential investors, and management: "If you want to invest in us, here are our terms."

Another aspect is the difference between long-term and short-term versions of shareholder theory. To recall two central messages from the CEOs who were interviewed: (1) All of them perceived ethics as a competitive advantage; and (2) the long-term perspective is more important than the short-term perspective.

In the long term, qualities like reputation, good will, brand name, and social capital have real value. The difficulty is getting through the short-term period first, and in addition measuring the economic value of reputation and goodwill is notoriously difficult in this initial stage. Thus, there is a balancing act in performing the duties to the economic expectations of the shareholders while constantly upholding ethical standards.

A long-term perspective is of course more than a boardroom issue. The message that the long term matters needs to be communicated throughout the company. To quote a sales representative:

> I think in sales you quite naturally have a conflict between a short-term strategy and long-term strategy. A top-down message is essential in a sales company, as you have people new to the business world, and their main motivator may be financial gain. They're very quick to think, "OK, what's the quick win here? How can I make this quick sale in order to put some money in my pocket?"[29]

Marketing and sales are departments where employees have a short-term incentive that may not necessarily reflect the long-term interests of the company. Another example is in the area of consulting. Here is a quotation from an employee working in the consulting industry:

> When I was on short-term engagements, there were often implementations that required coming up with a solution and implementing very quickly.
> This was often to the detriment of the client because we would come in, and we would implement a solution, and then we'd walk away. And they'd be left to continue with implementation, which sometimes they weren't prepared to do.
> On the other hand, the longer-term engagements, which involve multiple years of implementing a solution, allowed us to really nurture not only the solution itself but our relationship with the client.[30]

The economist Milton Friedman famously stated that if a manager uses shareholder money for his or her own personal viewpoint of what is good, the manager is essentially committing theft. It is not the manager's money. It is the shareholders' money. If the manager wants to make a philanthropic donation of his or her own money, that is fine. A manager should, according to Friedman, maximize profitability. He or she should distribute the resources or the profits to the shareholders, so the shareholders can then decide what they think is appropriate.

Friedman states that one should comply with the law, one should stay within the fair rules of competition, and one should consider the long-term reputation and goodwill of the company. All of this could apply to the examples provided by the CEOs participating in our survey.

There is another aspect of shareholder theory that is revealed in corporate legal history. Corporations are creations of society; the laws and rules concerning them change over time. As we noted earlier, Reuven Avi-Yonah, a law professor at the University of Michigan, has written an article that traces how the law has changed with respect to corporations, dating all the way back into Roman antiquity, and how it has evolved throughout society from a shareholder model to a stakeholder model.[31]

The important point is that the law changes. It is not static. If we were to go back in history to the time that the United States was founded, the only way in which businesses were able to obtain incorporation was to appeal directly to the legislature. That cumbersome step no longer exists, but now there is far more legal regulation of businesses than was the case in the early 1900s. The freedom of corporations to profit has been, and always will be, in a degree of flux.

The Volkswagen case mirrors these concerns. Though there was a short-term benefit in the software workaround strategy, it ended up imposing severe costs on the company for its violation of the law.

Stakeholder Theory The key originator of stakeholder theory was a professor at the Darden School at the University of Virginia named Ed Freeman. Freeman argued that all stakeholders should be treated as an end and not as a means to an end. They are not labor inputs. They are not interchangeable parts. They are human beings with their own ideas of good and bad. Freeman draws on the German philosopher Immanuel Kant, who developed what he called the "categorical imperative" and who arguably is the most influential philosopher in the Western world.

Kant's "categorical imperative" states that, to be a moral law, a law needs to be applied universally. In other words, we should be willing to apply any law or principle that we accept unto ourselves. How do we want to be treated? Do we want to be treated honestly? Compassionately? Fairly?

How then should corporations be operated? The answer is that they should be operated in such a manner that anyone who is affected by their corporate action is treated as an end. The people affected by these actions are called stakeholders because they have a stake in the company. Shareholders are also stakeholders. So too are employees, consumers, suppliers, local governments, national governments, and the environment. All decisions made by the corporation should take into consideration any person affected by its action. A stakeholder should be treated as an end and not as a means to an end.

The first step in applying stakeholder theory is to define who the stakeholders are. Who are the people, individuals, and organizations that are affected by the proposed corporate action? How should these stakeholders be prioritized? So many people are stakeholders that one has to find some mechanism of knowing who is most important at any particular time and place. To answer that question, the following formula could be applied. It is adapted from William (Bill) Frederick, a professor emeritus at the Katz School of Business at the University of Pittsburgh.

Bill characterized the stakeholder approach to business as EBB, or ethical business behavior, being a function of rights (particularly Kantian rights), plus justice (particularly Rawlsian justice), plus utilitarianism. So,

$$EBB = R_K + J_R + U$$

In this formula, Frederick characterized the way the field of business ethics generally attempts to prioritize certain stakeholders over others. Frederick favored a naturalist approach (that we used early in this book). Regardless of the critical dimension, Frederick accurately captured a way to describe today's leading components of stakeholder theory.

Rights Theory   The first element of stakeholder theory is rights. The primary expositor of "rights theory" is another professor of business ethics, Patricia (Pat) Werhane. She is concerned with emotive assertions and instead created a framework anchored by two different kinds of rights. One is a basic right (or a primary right), and the other is a secondary right (or a nonbasic right).

How does one know whether or not a stakeholder has a basic right? Werhane states that a basic right is something without which life would be intolerable. She claims that this includes life itself and some basic health needs, along with food, water, shelter, and freedom from torture.

One needs to ask whether a corporation can have an impact on an employee's life and health. Studies done in the 1980s, for example, examined battery restoration. To restore a battery, the accumulated lead acid must be dumped and then refreshed. This work was outsourced from the United States to Taiwan, and investigators found factory workers in Taiwan working knee-deep in lead battery acid. This has been shown to result in congenital defects among the workers' offspring, as well as various types of cancer in the workers themselves.[32]

Even if one could argue that the factory workers had known of these risks, the children born to them with health defects did not. This is one example of how corporations can have an impact on a person's health and life. The Volkswagen case provides another example, showing that the release of nitrogen oxide can damage the respiratory systems of those with asthma, emphysema, and bronchitis.

How do we define nonbasic rights? According to Werhane, these could include private property ownership. She states that people through history have been able to live happily and successfully without the right to private property. Looking back to hunter-gatherer times, there was a collective ownership of property, and people lived together and prospered. Thus, property and the right to income are examples of nonbasic rights.

If society does institute ownership of private property, then should we have laws that protect property interest? There should definitely be laws against trespassing. There should be laws against theft. Property should be protected. But, even in a society where there is private property, Werhane argues, in a case between a right to property, including corporate income, and a basic right of an employee's life or health, basic rights win.

There can even be a situation in which there is a contest between rights of equal stature: basic versus basic, secondary versus secondary. An example of two secondary rights that compete is in a labor dispute over pay levels between employees and employers. Both parties have rights to income. These are examples of equal nonbasic rights. In Werhane's model, one must come up with a compromise to try to honor both sides. Similarly, if one had basic rights of equal stature, which one would be more important? Again, both of them are essential, so a compromise is the only way forward.

An issue that often arises today concerns the environment. Does the environment have a basic right? Under Werhane's theory, the environment does not have a basic right because rights apply, again following a

Kantian analysis, only to human beings. However, she states that since human beings can be very much affected by environmental degradation, then derivatively one should protect the environment because ultimately human beings, and their basic rights, are affected by it.

Others claim that the environment is imbued with basic rights. Then, Earth itself would have basic rights to be protected in and of itself, as well as derivatively because of the negative impact that environmental degradation would have on others. The Volkswagen case again provides evidence of this with release of chemicals affecting global warming and acid rain.

If one still has not been able to resolve the dilemma, then one needs to find the formulation that creates the least harm to an affected stakeholder. Looking at the issues of jobs and labor disputes, it may well be that property rights (and derivatively, then, the rights to income) are secondary rights. A person laid off from a job will be adversely affected. Is there a way to create a lesser amount of harm to the employee in the process of laying off? It may well be that the company must reduce costs to stay in business, or it may be true that the employee is not doing the job well. But a company could be viewed as kinder by giving notice to the person that a layoff will occur, by providing funds for retraining, or by laying the person off in a way that is respectful rather than one that is demeaning. All of these examples would create less harm.

Justice Theory.   The second element within stakeholder theory is "justice." There are different elements of justice theory. One focuses on equality: equal people with equal talents and equal opportunities ought to be paid and treated equally. For instance, men and women who have the same educational skills and work experience should be paid the same. There is an injustice if they are not. This is an example of an equality version of justice.

A second kind of justice, distributive justice, is articulated well by the American philosopher John Rawls. Rawls states that people want to be treated fairly. We all have different ideas of what fairness means. So how do we know whether something is fair?

Rawls conceived of a social contract in which people might determine that societal rules were fair.[33] Using psychological studies of risk assessment, Rawls asked the following: if people did not know in advance what characteristics they would have when born (rich or poor, clever or less intelligent, attractive or less attractive), how would they know how they would want society to be constructed? He concluded that human beings would want to make sure that the most vulnerable members of society would be protected. In our case, people would want to be protected from corporate abuse.

Take, for instance, the example of the sales/account representative from a recruiting firm for quantitative Wall Street traders, who identifies her clients as those who are in a vulnerable position and who trust on recruiters to look out for their well-being:

> For my company in the recruitment world, we've got our client, and we've got our candidate. Candidates are our product—we essentially sell a set of skills and someone's resume to our client and place them in their next job and place of work.
>
> They're trusting us to liaise with our client and represent their skill set; represent the technical skills they have, in addition to the softer skills; and understanding their motivations of why they're looking to take the next step in their career. What's important to them? And what's critical to them in their next job that they take?[34]

Two prominent expositors of social contract theory in the field of business ethics are Tom Donaldson and the late Tom Dunfee from the Wharton School of Business. They created "Integrative Social Contracts Theory." This is a complicated theory of business ethics that combines a philosophical social contract (akin to what Rawls proposes) and draws from both this abstract concept and the real social contracts in place throughout all human societies. Donaldson and Dunfee's approach tries to navigate a way to be respectful to local communities by leaving them free to make decisions that are appropriate for their era and culture, while also holding all societies to some basic philosophical demands of justice.[35] For example, different societies may have differing norms on whether it is appropriate to hire and to promote family members. Other cultures may have different understandings of what constitutes a gift that builds relationships and one that amounts to bribery. Donaldson and Dunfee want to respect the freedom of local cultures to define what is right for them while also arguing that all societies do condemn corruption, thereby serving as evidence that some norms seem universal.

Professor Linda Lim, an international business professor who did her dissertation on the plight of women workers, particularly in Southeast

Asia, expected to find that they felt abused in poor working conditions. Instead, she found that they were incredibly grateful for their jobs because they provided a much-needed income. She cautioned that when we are making judgments of what fair working conditions are, we should talk with the people who are working in them before making conclusions. In other words, Donaldson and Dunfee would argue that one cannot simply condemn sweatshop labor through Western eyes; one should listen to the perspective of local culture. At the same time, there may be such egregious treatment that the violation of basic rights does require universal condemnation.

Dealing with vulnerable stakeholders can create leadership challenges. As senior ethics consultant Ellen Mignoni says:

> Businesses are working with probably the most vulnerable members of society around the world right now. And I think the way that they have been able to be successful is to make sure that they have the right partners who can deliver the right services at the right time that will really have an impact. Companies are much more focused on the kinds of partnerships they develop. They want to know the strength of the organization. They want to see the results that they are having, and they want to be able to measure those results.
>
> Companies don't have the resources (they don't need to be having the resources) or the expertise to solve social issues. They can work with partners who can deliver.[36]

Utilitarianism   The third framework is utilitarianism: the greatest good for the greatest number. Utilitarians like Bentham and Mill stated that "we all have different preferences," which they measured in an abstract unit called *utiles*. One person has one preference, and another person has another preference. So how do we decide which is more valuable? We cannot. But we can take such actions that tend to make the most people the happiest, as often as we can (a utilitarian decision).

Capitalism invokes certain utilitarian dimensions by attempting to create additional profits and to generate additional economic growth. Democracy is an example of utilitarianism where the greatest good for the greatest number is measured through votes. The party with the most votes—another kind of utile—wins office.

Utilitarian thinking is widespread in our society today (the majority wins, and the minority loses). Thus in a utilitarian decision-making process, there is some sort of protection for the rights of minorities. The Bill of Rights was created to protect freedom of religion, freedom of speech, and other such individual freedoms.

The corporate application of utilitarianism frequently is similar to long-term shareholder value. If the corporation takes care of all its stakeholders, this provides the greatest good for the greatest number of people. This will probably create the kind of goodwill, reputation, and social capital that will end up benefiting the corporation in the long run. The Volkswagen case demonstrates this model, with the scandal having an impact on the health of stakeholders and the well-being of the environment; therefore, given the anger against the company and the regulatory prosecution, the scandal will possibly affect the longer-term reputation, goodwill, and profitability of the company as well.

Having said this, one may not always find such a correlation of these theories. Rights theory and justice theory often oppose utilitarian theory. Rights and justice theories may also oppose shareholder theory.

Virtue   Human beings are social beings with consciences. When people live together there are certain rules of behavior to follow to stay in a relationship with others. We can apply this to business organizations as well. Businesses are communities. People can adapt their behavior to be a member of such a community.

Indeed, most of the examples cited by the CEOs revolve around an ethical identity and culture that had been established by the company in question long before a dilemma occurred. Whether that was J&J, the municipality of Copenhagen, or Mattel, the entity's own identity as an organization was at stake when the dilemma occurred. The company drew on that identity to resolve the problem. Other companies set out to create an identity that is appropriate for them going forward. This includes Maersk Shipping's new environmental focus or Starbucks and its renewed emphasis on quality.

Culture and identity are crucial to virtue theory, which is why these dimensions, especially interwoven and grounded in sincerity, merit their own treatment in the next chapter. They demonstrate that people remain influenced by the community—here in the context of the company in which they work.

An article in the *Academy of Management Journal* several years ago called "Monkey See, Monkey Do" analyzed how people mimic the behavior they see at work so they can fit in. A virtue approach recognizes that, and it recognizes that there will be certain behaviors that are championed and others that are disapproved of. And if we are more mindfully aware of what those behaviors are, then we can practice the behaviors that we really value, as opposed to the ones that are introduced but are not important or particularly good.

To apply virtue theory, one identifies the relevant virtues, defines them, and then applies them. And by doing so, one is fitting in to a larger naturalistic dimension of human nature that has a dialectic going back and forth between individual and community. It is hard to imagine a group of people believing that virtues such as honesty and accountability are not crucial in business. They can be found along with the other virtues identified by the CEOs we surveyed.

STEP SEVEN: CONCLUSION

After all the analysis, what are the decisions to be made? This could be to choose the justice approach in the stakeholder theory. It could be to choose maximizing profitability in the short term. It could be a mix of a variety of the frameworks.

These steps provide a rigorous method of making clear and thoughtful decisions. The final step to be added concerns corporate culture and the importance of sincerity in forming that culture.

6 Building on Good Decisions with Authenticity and Sincerity

There is a cluster of terms that surround honest and frank communication that seem readily applicable to business: integrity, consistency, coherence, authenticity, and sincerity, to name a few. How fine of distinctions do we need to make among these terms?

In this chapter, we take a middle-ground approach. We want to articulate the importance of authenticity and sincerity, so that we know what they mean in a business context and also how they have an impact on business life. In the first section, we define what we imply when using these terms; in the second section, we discuss the impact this has on business life and why authenticity and sincerity are crucial virtues important for business today.

Sincerity and Authenticity

When people use the term *sincerity* today, we believe they mean that a person is truthful, honest, and transparent. However this is not the way philosophers have treated the term for the last two hundred years.

According to the German philosopher Hegel, sincerity is "the heroism of dumb service" because a sincere person attempts to uncritically conform to the expectations and norms dictated by society. Hegel's criticism was rooted in the arguments of the Protestant Reformation, where sincerity was used to describe a person who adhered to a "true" doctrine; the term was only rarely attributed to one's individual conscience.[1] Instead, the word Hegel used to describe the notion of being true to oneself was *authenticity*, a concept closely related to sincerity.[2]

The famous Renaissance political theorist Machiavelli used sincerity very differently. In his sixteenth-century political advice to those running the emerging state, he argued that appearing sincere is a good idea—it gains moral and political support from people—but actually being sincere is a naïve approach.[3] In the early 1970s, Lionel Trilling stated that "the word sincerity has lost most of its former high dignity . . . When we hear it, we are conscious of the anachronism which touches it with quaintness . . . If we speak it, we are likely to do so with either discomfort or irony."[4]

Despite these criticisms, the general idea of sincerity remains today. Regardless of the term used, its core definition is still valued. In his history of the term, Magill acknowledges that sincerity and authenticity, ideals that "insist you say what you feel and be true to who you are in order to live a satisfying life" remain tremendously powerful.[5] *Authenticity* may be the term used more for the value of internal integrity and truthfulness,[6] but critics have attacked this as well, arguing that authenticity could also support narcissism.[7]

Recognizing that there are philosophical nuances, critiques, and histories embedded in these terms, it seems that there is a commonsense notion of the value of sincerity and authenticity insofar as they command a moral stance of knowing ourselves (Socrates' position) and an ability to communicate that self to others.[8]

Two key thinkers—one a Danish theologian (Søren Kierkegaard) and the other a German philosopher (Martin Heidegger)—describe the self in relation to others. That is, in becoming truly our "selves," we do so in relation with other people or other things; we do not do so in isolation from them.[9] Charles Taylor, a twentieth-century Canadian political philosopher, among others, has more recently reclaimed the notion of authenticity, formulated as an ability to articulate an identity—indeed, to even transcend what we think of our "selves" as being—and that we do so in relationship to a "good" and to one's membership in a community.[10]

One could elaborate much more extensively on these themes, and the philosophically astute reader will see that there are nuances, histories, and distinctions that do bear elaboration. We do not wish to join this debate, although we do want to acknowledge the existence of this philosophical nuancing. At the same time, a business reader may well ask, why do we need to do this at all?

The reason is that these notions of authenticity and sincerity have their place in the business lexicon. Returning to Magill's extensive analysis of sincerity, he criticizes a business application of authenticity's importance. He says:

> In 2007, Harvard Business School Press published a book called *Authenticity: What Consumers Really Want*, by James H. Gilmore and B. Joseph Pine II. There we learn why companies need to harness the power of authenticity and why it has become so powerful as a "sector strategy." Most people want "what is real," the authors said, because they see so much fakeness and phoniness around them. This thirst makes consumers vulnerable to being convinced that anything can be authentic. As Gilmore and Pine see it, authenticity is not a real quality of things or people. Rather, everything is authentic, and there is "no such thing as inauthentic experience because experiences happen inside of us." By this logic, all experiences are just as equally inauthentic.
>
> In order to capitalize on this, "business . . . can gain the perception of authenticity [and can render their inauthentic offerings as authentic.]" So much more fakeness and phoniness. All you need is a few tricks up your sleeve (stonewash, the worn look, or simply the word "authentic" or "vintage" attached to your product) and presto: all things mass-produced, market-tested, and inauthentic (that is, things that lie about what they actually are) can be transformed into authentic products. It's no wonder we doubt the reality of authenticity.[11]

This criticism lays bare the core problem of authenticity. At least some have co-opted it into a gimmick; the same can hold true for sincerity as well. The core problem, as Magill sarcastically claims, is that if authenticity is simply something that any given individual claims, then there's not much to it, and the idea becomes susceptible to the easiest of marketing (however cynical and insincere) strategies: "these jeans will let you be you."

This notion of authenticity seems far removed from what our CEOs told us about the importance of factors, virtues, and ethics in business articulated in Chapters 3 and 4. Nor does it align with our claims of an ethical content that might enhance trust, integrity, and culture.

Any of these terms—sincerity, authenticity, trustworthiness, integrity— can be window dressed, especially if any given individual can make the word mean what he or she wishes it to mean and perhaps even more so if it provides an advantage to that person in dealing with others. We believe that these terms can provide an advantage in working with others but not when used in a manipulative context. Although one can spin these terms into sound bite commercialism, one can also use the core idea of these terms for mutual advantage.

Given its ethical connotations, Magill states that sincerity is more at home in religion, art, philosophy, and literature rather than in politics.[12] He does not even mention business, but we believe there is much to be gained by companies and their leaders by practicing sincerity. Being sincere is not about a CEO or other senior director portraying empathy, though this would be convincing. Being able to project sincerity will work only when there is a foundation of action that makes emoting and head-on frankness credible.

Authenticity and sincerity fit in with our surveyed CEOs' opinions that decisions be made on a long-term basis rather than on short-term opportunism. Corporate sincerity and authenticity rest on a company believing that a certain course of action is the right thing to do and doing it over an extended period of time. They are the products of historical actions and not corporate marketing gimmicks.

A company deciding today that it will be authentic tomorrow has missed the point. Becoming authentic takes a lot of time, effort, and continuous dedication, and a company may achieve this only over the course of many years. In other words, the decision for a corporation to be authentic and sincere cannot be made lightly or halfheartedly.

We believe that sincerity and authenticity are valued by customers, employees, suppliers, and other stakeholders. Companies that adopt sincerity and authenticity as a way of interacting with these stakeholders will engender trust. That itself is a good thing to be pursued independently, exactly as our CEOs suggested—that acting on the basis of values is an independent good.

Trust is also necessary. Many economists have argued this. Trust reduces monitoring and transaction costs. Fellow contractors (employees, customers, suppliers, and the like) are willing to engage in more business with those in whom they repose trust. Moreover, trust can increase business activities themselves.[13]

The reason people are willing to do more business with those in whom they repose trust is exactly because those individuals pursuing trustworthy activities are treating that trustworthy conduct as an independent good. It does make them more money. But what really enhances trust is when one knows that a contracting partner believes that promise keeping, honesty, and being sincere are all the right things to do. These behaviors, apart from the financial consequences, are more economically valuable than undertaking the same values for their economic, reputational value.[14]

Individuals and Companies

Companies may have no souls, but the individuals that comprise them do. Moreover, although companies may be "persons" in a legal sense,[15] they are not in an ethical sense with respect to concepts such as sincerity and authenticity. Yet, just as the CEOs we surveyed had no difficulty citing both exemplary and problematic actions and readily ascribed moral virtues and failings to company actions, we perceive companies as being sincere and authentic because they are relational "persons." They interact with an array of stakeholders who have perceptions and make judgments about the company. In this respect, companies are not that different from individuals. A way to see this is to see what happens when a company undertakes an initial public offering (IPO).

From an ethical perspective, IPOs have often been criticized for their problems, especially with respect to conflicts of interest.[16] Investment analysts conduct due diligence to make sure a company is ready for public markets while possibly retaining some shares that they will recommend for favored clients, who can cash in once the IPO takes place. Entrepreneurs could benefit from hiding or minimizing company faults to obtain higher stock prices.

At the same time, an IPO is also a unique time to institutionalize the practices that entrepreneurs value. It is not unusual for a closely held company to have a strong sense of family-oriented values, values that the founding family holds and by which the private company operates. The risk of being publicly owned is that investors are much more likely to simply invest for monetary return than to support historical values, and so the family's values can be deprioritized in an IPO.[17]

As a way to handle this, many companies will state the company's beliefs and values at the time it goes public. This is exactly what Johnson & Johnson did in the 1940s when it articulated the already-mentioned Credo. It is also what companies such as Timberland, Starbucks, and Whole Foods did at the time of their IPOs. They stated the values by which the company would operate so that a potential investor who wanted to invest in the company would know that this was the way the company operated.

Research consistently shows that, in the long term, there is an economic benefit to companies behaving ethically. Whether this is embedded in the terms of "good ethics is good business," or whether corporate financial performance and corporate social performance are linked, empirical evidence shows that there is value in conducting business exactly the way the CEOs we surveyed indicate.

In a novel empirical study, researchers looked at the language used in IPOs. How often did the IPO documents mention terms such as honesty, integrity, and trust? Then the researchers tracked how well the companies performed. Currently their data are over a three-year period of time, with new research extending that time period. The results show that the companies that spend the time portraying their corporate values tend to fare well both on corporate responsibility indices and also on corporate performance measures compared to other companies that did not.[18]

More specifically, the study tracked terms such as *authenticity, integrity, trust, promise keeping,* and *mission statements* in their corporate S-1 securities filing documents. Tracking CSR scores, companies that included these terms scored higher both one year and three years after the IPO. These CSR scores have also been correlated with financial performance scores,[19] which suggests that companies that have made genuine commitments to these values are recognized and valued financially by investors. (The authors would like to note that there could be other interpretations of these preliminary results, and the study remains in its early stages).[20]

At the same time, the study suggests that companies that identify who they are—a core feature of authenticity—and then sustain those values over time—a core feature of sincerity—fare well both reputationally and economically.

Purpose provides an independent anchor for sincerity and authenticity. Of course, a business will be interested in making money. But its commitment to an independent good is where it claims its ethical opportunities and constraints and also its claim for doing something for the benefit of society. We have seen examples of exactly this in Chapter 4 with exemplary companies such as Johnson & Johnson, Starbucks, Maersk, Mattel, and so on, and we have seen how such an independent purpose was not present in Chapter 3's problematic examples of Enron, Stewart, Lehman Brothers, and Firestone.

A company can be authentic about pursuing a good independent of its economic value. It can be sincere in communicating this desire and how it goes about pursing this. This, of course, can be true of a small own-ership company where the limited number of shareholders can provide a focus for the entire company. Ferring Pharmaceuticals is an example of this, where the chairman of the board, Frederik Paulsen, insists on a standard of ethical conduct throughout the organization. Those compa-nies that, through their IPO, announce how they will achieve this have a similar opportunity. It may be more complicated for the reason Saxegaard suggests, but the clarity of a company's commitment, even when public, can create that independent purpose.

Much more difficult is the job of a CEO of a publicly held company that does not have this history of purpose-driven conduct. It may still be possible through strong leadership and/or when there is desire and moti-vation to change, but there will be challenges. Like some human beings, companies may have mixed motives. Most of us desire both profit and purpose, and keeping those two things in balance can be a challenge. This is especially true given the psychological biases we detailed in the previous chapter. We can easily be blinded by our own biases. Another challenge is conflicting stakeholders. Suppliers and environmental activists may not have the same idea of the company's purpose. The same holds true for customers and employees or any other dyad of stakeholders with differing interests.

Sincerity and Companies

To recall from earlier chapters, the leading eight factors the CEOs identified as being very important or important for ethical organizations were

1. "Tone at the top"
2. Listening to all stakeholders
3. Long-term focus
4. Clear policies and legal compliance
5. Matching rhetoric and rewards
6. Proving commitment, especially in a crisis
7. Values practiced at work contributing to a better local environment
8. Continuous improvement on and attention to values and how they may change

We benefit from what the CEOs, board members, and scholars tell us, but we believe that we can offer some additional insights that might be valuable in creating corporate cultures that incorporate sincerity and authenticity and that have not yet been regularly practiced.

If sincerity and authenticity are important—indeed, if they provide an edge—then how do we cultivate these qualities? This is particularly important to consider because of the communal nature of a company. A company is not just one person, but if sincerity and authenticity most directly interface with individuals, it may make sense that companies provide the opportunity for individuals to achieve their own authenticity and sincerity in their work. This is exactly the strategy of Whole Foods, where Mackey states that his company's model is not only to pursue an entrepreneur's purpose but that, in every person's job, they have the opportunity to pursue whatever purpose they bring to work with them.

This suggests an overlapping need for a richer corporate culture, along the lines we discussed in the opening chapters and supplemented with this chapter's notions of sincerity and authenticity. We suggest that four additional factors drive a company toward an organization where sincerity and authenticity can flourish exactly because it is a place where this shared, communal dimension exists.

BOARD ENGAGEMENT

Although "tone at the top" will always be important and will always prioritize the work of the senior management, boards of directors increasingly have legal responsibilities for oversight of company ethics and compliance programs. It sends a strong message throughout the company if the importance of the factors and values identified by senior management are not only their message but that of the collective body of the institution's corporate governance.

Two particular functions may be important in this respect. First, are these issues discussed at the board level? Second, are there board members who actively oversee and engage with company personnel in assessing ethical actions? Board engagement substantiates an authentic dimension of ethics and responsibility as a core feature of a company. Board engagement also conveys a message of sincerity that these issues are, in fact, important to the company and that they are taken very seriously.

Table 6.1. Ethics versus compliance comparison

Ethics	Compliance
Prevention	Detection
Principles-based	Laws/rules-based
Values-driven	Fear-driven
Implicit	Explicit
Spirit of the law	Letter of the law
Discretionary	Mandatory

One way that boards can have an impact on the company and its attention to both compliance issues and ethical concerns is to clearly differentiate between the two, as exemplified in Table 6.1.

The board's independent commitment to each of these areas amplifies the tone at the top and provides for increasing institutionalization and embedding of both ethics and compliance while also helping to avoid conflating them.

STORYTELLING

The most natural way for people to talk about ethics is to tell stories. Philosophical principles, legal rules, and psychological biases aside, people tend to relate better to personal stories. This is one of the features of reading a book or watching a movie: we expect there to be a moral to a story.

In several consulting engagements, as well as with thousands of students over three decades, Professor Fort has assigned a paper where participants are asked to tell a story about something they saw in business that they thought was good. Most people can think of any number of things that might annoy them, but it is harder to clearly state what one thinks is good and then to defend it.

Nevertheless, this assignment gets to the heart of what employees (and potentially other stakeholders) believe is ethical and important. Companies should encourage employees to share their stories with others with whom they work.

Storytelling lies within what is often called narrative ethics. The idea is that each person or organization has a historically developed identity.

Narrative expresses that history and identity and also portrays where the person is at a given time and place within that history.

Often, ethics is simply not discussed in business. A survey done years ago concluded that most people do not talk about ethics at work because there is a fear that ethics talk is "soft," and one only gets ahead in business by being "tough."[21] As a result, ethics often is not discussed at all unless there is a scandal or dilemma, at which point it may be too late. Avoiding the subject does nothing to create awareness or build skills in decision making, nor does it help to create an affective culture of sincerity and authenticity.[22] Storytelling provides a way for people to discuss what they think is important and invites further discussion along these lines.

SKIN IN THE GAME

A philanthropic approach or corporate social responsibility regime is a decision of strategy at the highest levels of the company. However, to engage all the members of an organization, companies may implement corporate responsibility approaches that allow employees to identify the organizations that might deserve corporate attention, or they might allow employees to volunteer their time to causes that mean the most to them.

Timberland, for example, gives its employees forty hours a year to volunteer for charitable activities of the employees' choice.[23] Such company support of employee engagement sends a strong signal to employees that the company values social and ethical engagements beyond making a financial donation. It asks employees to sincerely engage with social values that relate to their work.

This approach shares much with what is sometimes called Values-Based Management.[24] Values-based management approaches have existed for a long time in human resources circles, and one of the authors has elaborated on this approach in the pharmaceutical industry.[25] Many companies invest in getting their managers to also be good people managers, who listen to their employees and help them maximize their potential. There will always be situations that are not described in the company manual; therefore, it is preferable that management generates the company's values for employees and that employees take these values into careful consideration in the way they conduct themselves and their work on a day-to-day basis. This is an "empowering-of-managers" approach that corresponds to placing greater responsibilities on individuals and taps into employee motivation and interest in learning.

Values-based training does not happen in a vacuum. If one seeks to integrate a values-based approach throughout a company, logic dictates that the most powerful elements of the company must be involved. This means senior management involvement. The old adage that ethics starts at the top is true, but if a values-based approach is to be institutionalized, it cannot depend solely on the views of any one person. This means that an integrated approach must also involve the board of directors.

During one of the author's services on the board of directors of Ferring Pharmaceuticals, senior management at Ferring appointed an independent global ethics officer to take overall responsibility for ensuring that the philosophy and the principles behind the company are known and applied actively in all Ferring divisions. This work is organized through an ethics and compliance committee, which reports directly to the board of directors. The day-to-day work is carried out from the ethics office, and its remit is to disseminate awareness of these principles and values throughout the organization and to train and underpin each individual employee's integrity.

In many companies, work with ethical guidelines and compliance are consolidated into a single function, and the company implements a common and coordinated effort. In such cases, the compliance function often has the greatest influence because it is easier to comply with something devised by a regulatory authority. Ferring believes that the two functions of ethics and compliance should be worked on in parallel. These two functions report together to a board committee. Ferring places intense focus on the ethical component in its own right while ensuring that individuals are trained and supported in making the right decision in difficult situations.

When there is "skin in the game," individuals throughout the company engage their intellectual, moral, and emotional intelligences to make good decisions. Ethics must be embedded in the company so that the entire organization becomes values driven.

MEDIATING INSTITUTIONS

At the heart of ethics and ethical cultures are moral sentiments that feature humans' caring nature for others. [26,27] Some may characterize this as our human social nature,[28] whereas others may go further and call it a moral aspect of our human nature.[29]

Genetic relationships may be one way to engender a caring culture, but sociologically the important dimension is not family per se but running a business as a *mediating institution*. This sociological term includes families as well as other small institutions where there is face-to-face engagement, a closeness, so that individuals experience consequences of moral actions and thereby gain moral character.[30] This experience matters most when there is a long-term relationship with others; such a historical relationship accentuates the need to take into account the consequences of one's actions.

Natural law theorists have long relied on this concept to claim that these mediating institutions foster the development of moral character. Studies in archeology and neurobiology substantiate the point that human groups experience natural breaking points at group sizes with limits of 6, 30, 150 and, finally, 500. This concept has also been applied in great detail to businesses.[31] As population sizes grow larger, hierarchy tends to be relied on more, including in business.[32]

It is difficult for any person to concretely recognize that her or his actions have an impact on another person geographically far away. It is not impossible, especially with technology, but when we are in close, long-term, meaningful relationships with others, ethics tends to have a greater meaning.

This insight has implications for corporate culture. Creating the sizes of work groups and the internal structuring of an organization to match employees' neurological capabilities and sentiments of individuals can be an important tool in ensuring that a company acts as a mediating institution.[33] If workers work in small groups—where they experience direct consequences of their actions—then the virtues associated with relationships (honesty, truth telling, promise keeping, accountability, and so on) become more concrete and more important to daily interaction. In turn, this historical relationship tends to reinforce a culture in which ethics matters on a daily basis.

Conclusion

At the core of sincerity (and authenticity, trust, and integrity) resides an earnest effort in attempting to perform ethical values because those values are good in and of themselves. This sincerity is at the core of what our survey executives—sometimes in different words—told us is crucial to the optimal, ethical, and efficient functioning of their companies. The payoff for such conduct seems to be the greatest when the attempt to pursue ethics purely for its own value is the greatest.

Communicating this sincerity requires a long-term relationship—a historical relationship. It is not something simply concocted as a marketing attempt or sales pitch. One communicates sincerely by doing it honestly and repeatedly. One imbues sincerity within organizations through the factors articulated by the CEOs we surveyed and, we suggest, by incorporating the four additional measures we describe in this chapter. Companies that embrace this concept of sincerity and do it continuously with these twelve factors create a competitive edge derived from their trustworthiness in the marketplace.

7   Twelve Ways to Lead with
the Sincerity Edge

The good news about making sincerity and authenticity central to a company's work is that it is already being done, and research suggests that incorporating these traits provides a competitive edge over companies that do not. The fact that it is a competitive edge is, in large part, why it is being done. Every one of the CEOs we interviewed views ethics as having a competitive advantage. They do not see it as a constraint that prevents them from competing in the market. This is important because conventional wisdom might make one think that ethics is fine and nice to have, but business is rough and tough with no time for such fineries.

Interestingly, viewing sincerity as having a competitive edge can hide the paradox of why and how sincerity is important. Sincerity and authenticity, like virtues such as honesty, loyalty, accountability, and integrity, have their own value as independent goods. As we saw, the economist F. A. Hayek realized this too: ethical conduct builds trust, which supports business transactions. What is most *efficient*, Hayek believed, was not the proof of their economic value but that these goods need to be pursued for their own independent value. When pursued in that way they became, paradoxically, more effective than when they were pursued because they were efficient.

Sincerity makes this happen. Sincerity calls for us to pursue virtuous behaviors simply because they are good things to do. If we sincerely pursue them, they have their greatest economic payoff. As our survey shows, executives already realize and practice this approach. It is not wishful thinking; this is the way great businesses already work.

The bad news about making sincerity and authenticity central to a company's work is that it is tough. It can be hard to be authentic continuously. It takes effort to maintain integrity continuously. One of the reasons that the assignment given to students—to write a story about something that is good in business—is hard is because it forces us to think deeply about who and what we are and what we believe in and are willing to stand up for.

The same holds true, perhaps even more complexly, with companies as well. Rather than just one individual, companies are comprised of hundreds and thousands of individuals. Determining how they come together collectively through a company's leadership, history, and culture, so that an authentic identity may be understood and practiced, is also hard work. Being able to sincerely communicate that identity imposes another difficult step. Thus, in trumpeting the importance of sincerity, authenticity, and other ethical values and in assuring readers that successful businesses often already implement them, we do not suggest that this is easily done. It is hard work.

Accepting the challenge of hard work does not seem an obstacle to those who readily embrace the importance of the sincerity edge. After we concluded our interviews, we asked another CEO to review the results. Old National Bank (ONB) is the largest financial institution headquartered in the state of Indiana, with more than US$12 billion in assets and branches in four Midwestern states. Ethisphere Institute has named ONB as one of its top ethical companies in the United States for four years in a row, so it seems the company has embraced this challenge.

One of the challenges of being a corporate ethical activist is the risk of becoming a target in the crosshairs of some corporate wrongdoing, no matter how small. For example, in 2001, Professor Fort learned of the actions of an exemplary company, cited for other good actions previously in this book. He invited company representatives to campus to give a talk because he thought their work in a poverty-stricken area of South America would inspire his students. The company executives politely declined, saying that while they were proud of their work and would continue to do so, they believed that the more they trumpeted their actions, the more of a target they would become for an aspiring critic.

How, then, does a company weigh the edge afforded by authenticity and sincerity and ethical behavior against the increased scrutiny that such a position invites? When this question was posed to Bob Jones, the CEO of Old National Bank, he mulled over this question and said the following:

> That is the challenge and the opportunity. That's the leadership responsibility you take if you are going to set off on an ethical course. I'm not going to brag about our good works, but I'm not going to hide them either, and I'd hope that, by our doing these things, other companies would see what is possible for them to do. If people want to find a flaw in us, they may find one. We're not perfect. But we accept the challenge of living up to what we say we want to be.[1]

Being a potential target is not the only challenge. As we have reported throughout the book, in the long term, ethical conduct does have a pay-off, especially when business people pursue ethics as having its own independent value apart from that payoff. The short-term view, however, is more difficult. Actions that may benefit the company in the long term may not necessarily possess a positive quantitative return on short-term investment. Especially for publicly held companies under the pressure of frequent earnings targets, employees committed to the long-term value of ethics and to ethics itself have another challenge to navigate. Jones attempted to respond to this question as well:

> Well, you have to have a thick skin. And you have to constantly communicate what you are doing to the investors and to the board and to the other stakeholders as well. Those communications have to be frank, but if we are honestly and continuously communicating to our stakeholders, especially in this case, our investors, then we believe we will have the investors who believe in our strategy.[2]

In researching this book, we have listened to business leaders, and we have reported and analyzed what they have had to say about important virtues and how to bring those values into play at work. We have added a few of our own examples where we think that, in situations where best practices are implemented, there are ways in which companies might go even further. Here is a recapitulation of those twelve factors:

1. *"Tone at the top"*: The sincere messages of senior management matter. This was clear in all the surveys conducted. Leadership matters. It was also clear in both the positive and the negative examples of company behavior identified by the CEOs. Those companies that

suffered scandals had poor leadership, whereas those that were exemplary always had a strong tone at the top.

In one of Professor Fort's interviews with an organization that has had significant legal trouble, the leader of the organization opined that he could not conceive of a relationship between leadership and ethics. It is little wonder this organization is in trouble.

How leaders express themselves makes a huge difference as corporate employees listen to what the CEO believes to be important. If the CEO does not stress the importance of the ethical ways the company carries out its business, the absence of value-driven concepts is noticed.

Yet, even if leaders get the rhetoric right, they also need to follow up on how decisions are made and the incentives that are created to encourage people within the company to accomplish the positive rhetoric used by the CEO. Sincerity is demonstrated when actions align with rhetoric.

2. *Listening to stakeholders:* Taking time to hear what the stakeholders have to say and either implementing recommendations or at least explaining why other actions are being taken is important. This has a primary application for shareholders, employees, customers, and suppliers. It has a secondary application to more distant stakeholders such as government, media, and activists. The companies that listened to their stakeholders, such as Starbucks or Maersk, were able to implement policies and programs that were widely admired and that motivated the workforce as well.

After all, one of our central messages is that businesses do not exist in a vacuum. Businesses are part of society, and members of society will make themselves heard, one way or the other. Stakeholders will protest if they are outraged by a company's actions or wrongdoing. In an age where individuals have access to social media and an ability to express themselves individually in ways previously unthought of, it makes far more sense to take the advice of the CEOs we interviewed who stressed that company executives remain in dialogue with their stakeholders. Dialogue means listening as well as talking. Sincerely listening to one's stakeholders is a key step in practicing corporate ethics and ensuring business success.

3. *Long-term focus:* Corporate strategies that are geared toward the long term are more likely to incorporate and practice the values associated with sincerity. Empirical studies have long shown that, in the long run, corporate financial performance is correlated with corporate social performance. Good ethics can be good business. These relationships are true in the long run. This is harder in the short term, which helps to explain why companies that suffered scandals usually had a short-term focus, whereas those that were named as exemplary consistently propounded a long-term orientation.

The short-term focus essentially claims that one can undertake an unethical action and get away with it. No one will notice or, at least, no one will negatively react to it. Our executives did not seem too confident that that was realistic in today's fast-moving communications world.

Instead, as Per Saxegaard implies, the business strategy most likely to succeed is what he calls being "businessworthy," which essentially is to sincerely interact with society over the long term.

4. *Clear policies and legal compliance:* Companies gain trust when they follow applicable laws and when they clearly articulate policies for employees and other core stakeholders to follow. Research shows that these stakeholders are willing to follow a number of different policies as long as they are enforced and they are articulated, with top-level management not exempted from their application. Here again, the presence or absence of this feature was sharply delineated between the companies that suffered scandal and those lauded for exemplary behavior.

There is no one particular way to establish an ethics or compliance program in a company. Yet, one does need to be aware of social norms, and one best complies with legal and social expectations by the consistent and clear implementation of whatever policies and programs are established. There is certainly room for diversity and stylistic differences, yet consistency and clarity do remain a necessary constant for any program.

5. *Board engagement:* Empowering the board of directors to be an active force for values is an essential power devolvement that allows corporate culture to permeate the organization. Empowering the board makes values such as authenticity and sincerity real. It broad-

ens the scope of the parties who form the identity—and therefore the authenticity on which sincerity rests—and who comprise the company.

After the turn-of-the century scandals and the impending mortgage meltdown crisis a few years later, boards have been compelled to be more responsible to their oversight of the company. Because of legal pressures, board members are more engaged than in the past. They must be involved in more oversight of issues such as accounting provisions or executive compensation. This also creates the opportunity for boards to positively engage in reinforcing messages of authenticity, sincerity, and their relationship to business success. People look to the board today with more expectation than twenty years ago. As leaders of the company, along with the executives, they provide an important resource to tap.

6. *Matching rhetoric and rewards:* Most companies say they are going to do great things. No company promotes its faults. The question is whether hiring, firing, compensation, and other incentives in the organization match the rhetoric. If so, the likelihood of the organization being perceived as sincere increases, just as was seen in the exemplary examples. If rewards don't match rhetoric, the opposite occurs.

   It is probably impossible to find a company stating that it believes in unsavory conduct. Yet, employees will follow the incentive structures that companies establish, and if those structures push people toward shortcuts and dishonest actions, one can expect that shortcuts and dishonesty will follow.

7. *"Skin in the game":* Companies tend to tout their philanthropic engagement, often with large sums of money highlighted. These numbers can mask context and intent: Are they corporate window dressing, or do they suggest sincere engagement in philanthropic issues?

   Without minimizing the importance of philanthropy, which can indeed be a significant force for good, it does not take a lot of effort to write a check. It does not engage the passions, energy, sweat, and effort of many employees or others in the company.

   Donating not just money but time, energy, and effort enhances the sincere engagement of companies in their philanthropic efforts.

It creates personal relationships among the employees of a company and those they are working with. This might include relief efforts for victims of a natural disaster, tutoring and literacy programs in the community, local clean-up efforts, and building houses for the poor.

8. *Meaning it, especially when it counts:* In the final analysis, companies are most trusted when they are willing to stand behind their values even when it appears it will cost them money. The most inspiring cases came exactly when a company is faced with a serious problem. Until this is achieved, the odes to ethical conduct can be perceived simply as rhetorical devices. Actions speak louder than words.

   Johnson & Johnson's Corporate Credo might have been admired as a nice corporate mission statement, but it became lauded when it served as the basis for concrete action in a crisis. That is when the rhetoric proved sincere. The same could be said for the city of Copenhagen's actions with respect to Ryanair or Maersk's transformation to embracing sustainability practices.

9. *Storytelling:* The most natural way for people anywhere, including in business, to talk about ethics is to tell stories. What story can they tell that articulates their values? Providing employees, in particular, with the opportunity to share their stories (for instance, in small groups during periodic retreats) unleashes values talk in a way the laws and economic incentives never can. It also broadens the voices and the experiences of key stakeholders who make up the company, its culture, and its identity.

   An employee trying to make an ethical point, especially about an inspiring moment about a company practice, may look to a company policy, but it is much more likely that they will tell a story about some person who did something that inspired them.

   In an age of skepticism, where it is common practice to cast doubt on what seems to be good conduct, it is easy to hesitate to tell inspiring stories. But the CEOs had no difficulty finding them. Telling them so that people can see how good actions are possible in business can have a significant uplifting impact.

10. *Making companies mediating institutions:* Normative research argues that we inculcate moral values in small organizations where we experience the direct consequences of our actions. Empirical research

in neurobiology and primatology support this normative scholarship, suggesting that the way companies are structured makes a difference in employees' sense that they belong to an organization where values matter on a daily basis.

For better or worse, companies have cultures. Each company is a little different from another. Do employees believe that they belong at the company? Is it a place where their values are in tune with the company's values? Do they get a sense of satisfaction and meaningfulness at work? Do they feel they are respected and valued? Companies can have this impact on their employees and even with other stakeholders.

It is hard to imagine that alienated employees will make outstanding ethical choices for the benefit of themselves and in their role in the company. Yet those who are empowered and who see a fit between their values and those of the company are more likely to have the confidence and training to act on those values to make choices that benefit themselves and the company.

11. *"Sketching the bigger picture"*: Why is it necessary to be values driven? One reason is that it might make the world or the environment a better place, suggesting that there are bigger payoffs than one might expect in cultivating a sincere culture aimed at values-driven leadership and work.

The environmental movement has been a strong example of this. We believe that each one of our personal acts of recycling, for example, has an impact on our surroundings. And thus, when employees believe that their ethical actions can make a difference to society and are not simply isolated conduct one does at work, then they have a powerful reason to more mindfully—and sincerely—pursue ethical actions.

12. *Continuous improvement:* This concept, drawn from quality management, demands that any sincere leadership model constantly evolve, challenge itself, and pursue new knowledge.

Things change. Expectations evolve. Technologies revolutionize. We all have weaknesses that can be turned into strengths. All of these unavoidable factors of life mean that sincerely engaging in ethical conduct is not static, but instead that it requires ongoing attention and continuous attention and work.

This is true, for example, in the development of both social and environmental sustainability protocols and agreements that raise the bar for corporate conduct. From the Foreign Corrupt Practices Act and the UN Declaration on Human Rights to the EU Data Protection Regulation, the Global Reporting Initiative's Sustainability Reporting Guidelines, and the Paris Accord, among others, companies are asked to do more than they did in the past. There is little reason to expect that increases in the social demands placed on business will not continue so that ongoing improvement and adaptation will be necessary.

There will be businesses that engage in a downward spiral. The CEOs we surveyed identified a few of them. The ones they identified were caught out and have paid a price, both financially and with their reputations. There are many ways to be successful, to not only comply with the law but to be exemplary. The CEOs we surveyed identified several of these examples as well.

One has choices to make in the corporate world. What kind of businessperson are you? What kind of business do you manage? What kind of example do you set for others? What we found in our research and what we have put forward in this book is that there is a meaningful competitive edge in sincerely pursuing ethical values in business. And this is certainly very good news.

Notes

Chapter 1

1. The authors would like to acknowledge the assistance of several research assistants in preparing this article: Jason Allen, Mengxing Li, Chenxi Li, Christopher Oman, and Arturs Oganesjans.

2. Bill Ford, *We Can't Simply Sell More Cars*, N.Y. Times, July 7, 2014, available at www.wsj.com/articles/bill-ford-on-the-future-of-transportation-we-cant -simply-sell-more-cars-1404763769.

3. In early American legal history, incorporation was granted only when businesses demonstrated a social good that would occur through chartering; common examples included ferry services or the formation of municipalities. Reuven S. Avi-Yonah, *The Cyclical Transformations of the Corporate Form: A Historical Perspective on Corporate Social Responsibility*, 30 Del. J. Corp. L. 767 (2005).

4. See, for example, F. A. Hayek, *The Fatal Conceit: The Errors of Socialism* 47 (1988) (citing Hume's contention that the market creates incentive "even [for] bad men to act for the public good").

5. See, for example, R. Edward Freeman, *Strategic Management: A Stakeholder Approach* 240–242 (1984).

6. See R. Edward Freeman, *The Politics of Stakeholder Theory: Some Future Directions*, 4 Bus. Ethics Q. 409 (1994).

7. Thomas Moore, "The Fight to Save Tylenol," *Fortune*, Nov. 29, 1982, retrieved on October 7, 2012, from http://features.blogs.fortune.cnn.com /2012/10/07/the-fight-to-save-tylenol-james-burke/; see also Johnson & Johnson, "Our Credo," retrieved on January 26, 2014, from www.jnj.com/sites /default/files/pdf/jnj_ourcredo_english_us_8.5x11_cmyk.pdf.

8. Moore, *supra* note 7.

9. Id.

10. Id.

11. Judith Rehak, *Tylenol Made a Hero of Johnson & Johnson: The Recall That Started Them All*, N.Y. Times, Mar. 23, 2002, available at www.nytimes.com/2002/03/23/your-money/23iht-mjj_ed3_.html.

12. Id.

13. Id.

14. See, for example, PriceWaterhouseCoopers, *Do Investors Care about Sustainability? Seven Trends Provide Clues* (2012).

15. See Jacob Goldstein, *Putting a Speed Limit on the Stock Market*, N.Y. Times. Oct. 8, 2013, available at www.nytimes.com/2013/10/13/magazine/high-frequency-traders.html?_r=0.

16. Aspen Institute, *Overcoming Short-Termism: A Call for a More Responsible Approach to Investment and Business Management*, 2009, available at www.aspeninstitute.org/sites/default/files/content/docs/pubs/overcome_short_state0909_0.pdf.

17. David Tennant & Claremont Kirton, *The Impact of Foreign Direct Investment, Financial Crises and Organizational Culture on Managers' Views as to the Finance-Growth Nexus*, 41 J. Econ. Issues 625 (2007).

18. See, for example, Bill George, *Activists Seek Short-Term Gain, Not Long-Term Value*, N.Y. Times, Aug. 26, 2013, available at http://dealbook.nytimes.com/2013/08/26/activists-seek-short-term-gain-not-long-term-value/?_php=true&_type=blogs&_r=0.

19. See Joshua Daniel Margolis & James P. Walsh, *People and Profits? The Search for A Link between A Company's Social and Financial Performance* (2001).

20. Narjess Boubakri, Omrane Guedhami, & Oumar Sy, Corporate Governance and Ultimate Control, in *Institutional Approach to Global Corporate Governance: Business Systems and Beyond* 394 (J. Jay Choi and Sandra Dow, eds., 2008).

21. See Adam Smith, *The Theory of Moral Sentiments* (6th ed., 1790); available at www.ibiblio.org/ml/libri/s/SmithA_MoralSentiments_p.pdf; see also Patricia Werhane, *Adam Smith and His Legacy for Modern Capitalism* (1991).

22. Werhane, *supra* note 21, at 165.

23. Id.

24. Id. at 165–166.

25. See Hayek, *supra* note 4, at 39–40.

26. Id.

27. Id. at 41.

28. Id. at 13–14.

29. Id. at 74–75.

30. Robert Frank, *Passions within Reason* (1988).

31. Id. at 190.

32. Id.; see also Amy M. Schmitter, Hume on the Emotions, *Stanford Encyclopedia of Philosophy* (2006), retrieved on January 17, 2016, from http://plato.stanford.edu/entries/emotions-17th18th/LD8Hume.html.

33. Interview with David Rose on "The Moral Foundations of Economic Behavior," University of Missouri, St. Louis, EconTalk.org (Jan. 23, 2012), available at www.econtalk.org/archives/2012/01/david_rose_on_t.html.

34. Id.

35. Andrew Pollack, *Drug Goes from $13 a Tablet to $750, Overnight*, N.Y. Times (Sept. 20, 2015).

36. Chris Woodyard & Mary Jo Layton, *Massive Price Increase on EpiPens Raises Alarms*, USA Today (Aug. 25, 2016).

37. Susanne Stormer, *How Novo-Nordisk's Corporate DNA Drives Innovation*. (April 30, 2012), retrieved on January 11, 2017, from www.managementexchange.com/story/how-novo-nordisk's-corporate-dna-drives-innovation.

38. Michael E. Miller, *U.S. Indicts World Soccer Officials in Alleged $150 Million FIFA Bribery Scandal*, The Washington Post (May 27, 2015).

39. Owen Gibson, *Migrant Workers Suffering "Appalling Treatment" in Qatar World Cup Stadiums, Says Amnesty*, The Guardian (April 1, 2016).

40. Federal Reserve Board's Semiannual Monetary Policy Report to Congress before the House Committee on Financial Services, 107th Congress (2002) (statement of Alan Greenspan, Chairman, Federal Reserve), available at www.federalreserve.gov/boarddocs/hh/2002/february/testimony.html.

41. *See* James A. Thompson, *Greenspan for Dummies*, The Albion Monitor (May 17, 2002), available at www.monitor.net/monitor/0205a/copyright/greenspanfordummies.html, giving a former *Wall Street Journal* contributor's perspective on Greenspan and suggesting that Arthur Andersen's culpability may have been exaggerated.

42. See Andrea Newell, *Ben and Jerry's Social Mission*, TriplePundit (Apr. 18, 2013), available at www.triplepundit.com/2013/04/ben-jerrys-social-mission/.

43. See Charlie Kannel, *Corporate Responsibility Spotlight: Whole Foods Market*, The Motley Fool (Sept.14, 2012), available at www.fool.com/investing/general/2012/09/14/corporate-responsibility-spotlight-whole-foods-ma.aspx.

44. See Aman Singh, *Responsible Boots: A Peek into Timberland's Post-Merger Future*, Forbes (Aug. 2, 2011), available at www.forbes.com/sites/csr/2011/08/02/responsible-boots-a-peek-into-timberlands-post-merger-future/.

45. See Jacquelyn Smith, *The World's Most Ethical Companies*, Forbes (Mar. 6, 2013), available at www.forbes.com/sites/jacquelynsmith/2013/03/06/the-worlds-most-ethical-companies-in-2013/.

46. See Margolis & Walsh, *supra* note 19 at 8, 13.

47. Id. at 10–14.

48. Id.

49. Although a close study of this phenomenon is beyond the scope of this paper, consider campaigns on prominent social issues such as the civil rights movement.

50. Directive 2002/58, of the European Parliament and of the Council of 12 (July 2002) Concerning the Processing of Personal Data and the Protection of Privacy in the Electronic Communications Sector (Directive on Privacy and Electronic Communications), 2002 O.J. (L 201) 37 (EC), available at http://eur-lex .europa.eu/LexUriServ/LexUriServ.do?uri=CELEX:32002L0058:en:NOT.

51. Id.

52. Id.

53. Id.

54. Id.

55. See Deloitte, *Women in the Boardroom: A Global Perspective* (2011), available at www.deloitte.com/assets/Dcom-Tanzania/Local%20Assets /Documents/Deloitte%20Article_Women%20in%20the%20boardroom.pdf; see also Judith H. Dobrzynski, *How Women Are Getting on European Boards (and Why U.S. Companies Should Care)*, Forbes (Dec. 14, 2009), available at www .forbes.com/2009/12/14/norway-french-legislation-equality-forbes-woman -leadership-executive-boards.html (citing France's proposed legislation requiring 40 percent of boards be comprised of women).

56. See, for example, Kenneth R. Ahern & Amy K. Dittmar, *The Changing of the Boards: The Impact on Firm Valuation of Mandated Female Board Representation*, 127 Q. J. of Econ. 137, 147 (2012).

57. Although these numbers do appear impressive, there are reactions as well. Many Norwegian businesses privatized after the law took effect to avoid the requirement. Moreover, some have argued that, although the law may have increased the number of women in board seats, it has done little to increase the number of women in corporate executive positions. See Saleha Moshin, *Quota System Failing to Bridge Norway's Corporate Gender Gap*, Bloomberg News (Oct. 9, 2013), available at http://business.financialpost.com/2013/10/09 /quota-system-failing-to-bridge-norways-corporate-gender-gap/.

58. U.S Sentencing Commission, *U.S. Sentencing Guidelines Manual* (1984).

59. 524 U.S. 742 (1998).

60. Id. at 770 (citing *DeGrace v. Rumsfeld*, 614 F.2d 796, 805 [1980]).

61. *U.S. Sentencing Guidelines Manual.*

62. See, for example., Frank Navran & Edward L. Pittman, *Corporate Ethics and Sarbanes-Oxley*, Ethics Res. Ctr. (Dec. 31, 2003), available at www .ethics.org/resource/corporate-ethics-and-sarbanes-oxley; and Jesse Eisinger & Jake Bernstein, *Dodd-Frank Act: How Financial Reform May Be Going Wrong*, Bus. Ethics (June 5, 2011), available at http://business-ethics.com/2011/06/05/1821 -from-dodd-frank-to-dud-how-financial-reform-may-be-going-wrong/.

63. Robert Prentice, *Lessons Learned in Business School*, N.Y. Times (Aug. 20, 2002), available at www.nytimes.com/2002/08/20/opinion/20PREN.htmlex=.

64. Id.

65. Aneel Karnani, *The Case against Corporate Social Responsibility*, Wall St. J. (Aug. 23, 2010), available at http://online.wsj.com/news/articles/SB100014240 52748703338004575230112664504089.

66. Id.

67. Prentice, *supra* note 63.

68. See John C. Anderson, Manus Rungtusanatham, & Roger G. Schroeder, *A Theory of Quality Management Underlying the Deming Management Method*, 19 Acad. Mgmt. Rev. 472 (1994).

69. *See* Mark Starik & Gordon P. Rands, *Weaving an Integrative Web: Multilevel and Multisystem Perspectives of Ecologically Sustainable Organizations*, 20 Acad. Mgmt. Rev. 908 (1995).

70. Alexandra, Countess of Fredriksborg, & Timothy L. Fort, *The Paradox of Pharmaceutical CSR*, Bus. Horizons 151 (Mar.–Apr. 2014).

71. Id.

72. See L. S. Paine, *Value Shift: Why Companies Must Merge Social and Financial Imperatives to Achieve Superior Performance* (2003).

73. Id. at 111.

74. See Linda Klebe Treviño et al., *Managing Ethics and Legal Compliance: What Works and What Hurts*, 41 Cal. Mgmt. Rev. 131 (1999).

75. A. K. Nussbaum, *Ethical Corporate Social Responsibility (CSR) and the Pharmaceutical Industry: A Happy Couple?* Journal of Medical Marketing 9(1, 2009) at 67–76.

76. Id. at 25.

77. Eli Lilly & Company, 2011 Annual Report, Lilly.com (2012), available at http://investor.lilly.com/common/download/download.cfm?companyid =LLY&fileid=548541&filekey=E8FFDA89-5EC1-4D08-AB37-CD85F4 C0863D&filename=English.PDF.

78. Bayer, Annual Report 2012, Bayer.com (2013), available at www.bayer .com/en/annual-reports.aspx.

79. *About Us*, Medicines for Malaria Venture (2013), available at www.mmv .org/about-us.

80. UNEP, Partners for Youth and the Environment. UNEP.Bayer.com, retrieved on January 24, 2016, from www.unep.bayer.com/en/about-partnership .aspx.

81. See Bayer, *supra* note 78.

82. Pfizer, *Diflucan Partnership*, Pfizer.com, retrieved on January 21, 2016, from www.pfizer.com/responsibility/global_health/diflucan_partnership _program.

83. GlaxoSmithKline, *GSK Joins New Global Partnership to Help Defeat Ten Neglected Tropical Diseases by 2020*, GSK.com (January 30, 2012), available at www.gsk.com/en-gb/media/press-releases/2012/gsk-joins-new-global-partnership-to-help-defeat-ten-neglected-tropical-diseases-by-2020/.

84. Novartis, *Q&A about the Novartis MDT Leprosy Donation*, Novartis Foundation.org (2012), available at www.novartisfoundation.org/page/content/index.asp?MenuID=364&ID=1010&Menu=3&Item=43.2.4tis.

85. AstraZeneca, *AstraZeneca Young Health Programme (India) Annual Report*, YoungHealthProgrammeyhp.com (2013), available at www.younghealth programmeyhp.com/resources/programme-reports.

86. Boehringer Ingelheim, *Combating HIV/AIDS*, CorporateResponsibility. Boehringer-Ingelheim.com, retrieved on January 18, 2016, from http://corporate responsibility.boehringeringelheim.com/corporate_citizenship/combating_hiv_aids.html.

87. Bristol-Myers Squibb Foundation & National Network of Public Health Institutes, *Together on Diabetes U.S. Grantee Summit*, BMS.com (2013), available at www.bms.com/documents/together_on_diabetes/2013-Summit-pdfs/ToD-Program.pdf.

88. *Free Drug Programs*, Genzyme.com, retrieved on January 18, 2016, from www.genzyme.com/en/Responsibility/Patient-Access-to-Treatment/Humanitarian-Programs.aspx.

89. *Public–Private Partnership for Health Care in Tanzania*, AbbotFund .org (2013), available at www.abbottfund.org/project/17/67/Modernizing-Regional-Level-Labs-in-Tanzania.

90. *Annual Highlights 2011: Celebrating 25 years of the Mectizan Donation Program in 2012*, Mectizan.org (2011), available at www.mectizan.org/sites/www.mectizan.org/files/attachments/resources/Annual%20Highlights%202011%20English.pdf.

91. See Alexandra & Fort, *supra* note 70.

92. Nussbaum, *supra* note 75.

Chapter 2

1. John Mackey and Raj Sisodia, *Conscious Capitalism: Liberating the Heroic Spirit of Business* (2013).

2. Interview of Per Saxegaard by the author, June 3, 2015.

3. Johnson & Johnson, *Our Credo*, retrieved on January 26, 2014, from www.jnj.com/sites/default/files/pdf/jnj_ourcredo_english_us_8.5x11_cmyk.pdf.

4. BeKnowledge.com, *Human Resources Practices of Johnson and Johnson*, retrieved on January 8, 2016, from www.beknowledge.com/wp-content

/uploads/2011/01/16790Human%20Resources%20Practices%20of%20
Johnson%20and%20Johnson.pdf.

5. Id.

6. Thomas Moore, *The Fight to Save Tylenol*, Fortune (1982), retrieved on
October 7, 2012, from http://features.blogs.fortune.cnn.com/2012/10/07/the
-fight-to-save-tylenol-james-burke/.

7. See, for example, Katie Thomas, *New Recalls by Johnson & Johnson Raise
Concern about Quality Control Improvements*, N.Y. Times (Sept. 12, 2013), available at www.nytimes.com/2013/09/13/business/new-recalls-by-johnson-johnson
-raise-concern-about-quality-control-improvements.html?_r=0.

8. *In re Johnson & Johnson Derivative Litig.*, 900 F. Supp. 3d 467 (D.N.J.
2012).

9. Stipulation and Agreement of Settlement for *In re Johnson & Johnson Derivative Litig.*, *supra* note 8, available at www.millerchevalier.com/portalresource
/JJ_settlement.

10. *See* C. William Thomas, *The Rise and Fall of Enron*, J. of Accountancy
41, 41 (2002), available at www.journalofaccountancy.com/Issues/2002/Apr
/TheRiseAndFallOfEnron.htm.

11. See Theodore F. di Stefano, *WorldCom's Failure: Why Did It Happen?*,
E-Commerce Times (Aug. 19, 2005), available at www.ecommercetimes.com
/story/45542.html.

12. See Robert Lenzner, *Berni Madoff's US$50 Billion Ponzi Scheme*, Forbes
(Dec. 12, 2008), available atwww.forbes.com/2008/12/12/madoff-ponzi-hedge
-pf-ii-in_rl_1212croesus_inl.html.

13. Greg Smith, *Why I am Leaving Goldman Sachs*, N.Y. Times (Mar. 14,
2012), available at www.nytimes.com/2012/03/14/opinion/why-i-am-leaving
-goldman-sachs.html?pagewanted=all.

14. Charles Riley & Emily Jane Fox, *GlaxoSmithKline in US$3 Billion
Fraud Settlement*, CNN Money (Jul. 2, 2012), available at http://money.cnn
.com/2012/07/02/news/companies/GlaxoSmithKline-settlement/.

15. Kim S. Cameron & Robert E. Quinn, *Diagnosing and Changing Organizational Culture: Through the Competing Values Framework* (3d ed., 2011).

16. Id. at 14.

17. Id.

18. Id.

19. Id. at 15.

20. Id.

21. Id. at 16.

22. Id. at 16–17.

23. Id. at 17.

24. Id. at 16.

25. OCAI-Online, *About the Organizational and Cultural Assessment Instrument*, retrieved on January 27, 2016 from www.ocai-online.com /about-the-Organizational-Culture-Assessment-Instrument-OCAI.

26. See Cameron & Quinn, *supra* note 15, at 18 (citing Clyde Kluckhohn, Alfred Louis Kroeber, & Wayne Untereiner, *Culture: A Critical Review of Concepts and Definitions* [1952]).

27. See Cameron & Quinn, *supra* note 15, at 18.

28. Id. at 20.

29. Id.

30. Id.

31. Id.

32. Id. (citing *Organizational Climate and Culture* [Benjamin Schneider, ed., 1990]).

33. Bart Victor & John B. Cullen, *The Organizational Bases of Ethical Work Climates*, 33 Admin. Sci. Q. 101 (1988); but see Michelle Westermann-Behaylo, *The Relationship between Corporate Ethical Climate and Stakeholder Management* (Jan. 31, 2010) (unpublished PhD dissertation, George Washington University) (on file with author), available at http://pqdtopen.proquest.com/pqdtopen /doc/89184544.html?FMT=ABS.

34. *See* ECOA Study, *supra* note 126, at 12. ALMA: Please put unanswered au query in margin{AU: Which note are you citing here?—mp}

35. See OCAI-Online, *Organizational Culture Assessment Instrument* 5 (2010), available at www.ocai-online.com/userfiles/file/ocai_pro_example _report.pdf.

36. Id.

37. Id.

38. Id.

39. Id. at 7.

40. Id.

41. Id.

42. Id. at 6.

43. Id.

44. Id.

45. Id.

46. Id.

47. Id.

48. See Cameron & Quinn, *supra* note 15, at 139.

49. Id. at 24–25.

50. Id. at 25.

51. Id.

52. Id.

53. Id.

54. It is an open question, however, as to whether these values are "competing" or not. For example, values emphasizing harmony, on the one hand, and competition, on the other, may be able to be balanced with conscious effort. One could envision a sports team, for instance, that features stiff competition for playing time among players but with loyalty and cohesion still held together not only through a commitment to winning (a market value) but also by bonding among team members.

55. See Alexandra Countess of Fredriksborg & Timothy L. Fort, *The Paradox of Pharmaceutical CSR*, Bus. Horizons 151 (March–April 2014). Our reconceptualization aims not at claiming a definitive understanding of exact contours of such a graphic but to more impressionistically locate the tension among these values in a way that brings the "competing" values closer to a common language used by other culture theorists and also in a way that is embedded deeply within our very nature.

56. See, for example, William C. Frederick, *Values Nature and Culture in the American Corporation* 9 (1995).

57. Id.

58. Id. at 146.

59. Id. at 151.

60. See Timothy L. Fort, *Business, Integrity and Peace* (R. Edward Freeman et al., eds., 2007).

61. See Frederick, *supra* note 56, at 156.

62. Id. at 163.

63. Id. at 187–89.

64. Id. at 157–62.

65. Id. at 9.

66. Id. at 188–92.

67. Id.

68. Id. at 16.

69. Id.

70. See Cameron & Quinn, *supra* note 15, at 67 (using Apple as an example).

71. Id. at 8.

72. Id. at 67 (using Apple as an example).

73. Id.

74. Elliot D. Cohen, *You Are a Social Animal*, Psychol. Today (Sept. 21, 2010), available at www.psychologytoday.com/blog/what-would-aristotle-do/201009 /you-are-social-animal.

75. See, for example, Paul R. Lawrence, *The Biological Base of Morality?*, 4 Bus., Sci., and Ethics 59 (2004).

76. To be sure, it is true that this change could take a dark turn of change to unethical behavior and culture. Addressing that issue becomes the topic of another paper.

77. See Cameron & Quinn, *supra* note 15, at 2.

78. See, for example, Mackey & Sisodia, *supra* note 1, at 20.

79. Id. at 86.

80. Id.

81. Id.

82. See Cameron & Quinn, *supra* note 15, at 79.

83. Id.

84. Kristin Hahn, presentation at Professor Fort's Cultural Norms in Global Business Class (Feb. 2013).

85. Alex Berenson et al., *Despite Warnings, Drug Giant Took Long Path to Vioxx Recall*, N. Y. Times (Nov. 14, 2004), available at www.nytimes.com/2004/11/14/business/14merck.html?pagewanted=all&_r=0.

86. *Bristol-Myers Squibb to Pay More Than US$515 Million to Resolve Allegations of Illegal Drug Marketing and Pricing*, United States Department of Justice (Sept. 17, 2013), available at www.justice.gov/opa/pr/2007/September/07_civ_782.html.

87. Michael Schmidt & Katie Thomas, *Glaxo Agrees to Pay US$3 Billion in Fraud Settlement*, N. Y. Times (July 2, 2012), available at www.nytimes.com/2012/07/03/business/glaxosmithkline-agrees-to-pay-3-billion-in-fraud-settlement.html?pagewanted=all.

88. Gardiner Harris, *Psychiatrists Top List in Drug Maker Gifts*, N. Y. Times (June 27, 2007), available at www.nytimes.com/2007/06/27/health/psychology/27doctors.html.

89. See, for example, Joshua Daniel Margolis & James P. Walsh, *People and Profits? The Search for a Link between a Company's Social and Financial Performance* (2001); and Marc Orlitzky, Frank Schmidt, & Sara Rynes, *Corporate Social and Financial Performance: A Meta-Analysis*, 24(3) Organization Studies, 403–441 (2003).

90. Alexandra Christina, *The Essence of Trust in Business Today*, speech presented at the 2012 Business for Peace Summit, Oslo, Norway.

91. Tom Randall and David Voreacos, *Merck's Reserves US$950 Million for Vioxx Crime Probe*, Bloomberg.com (Oct. 29, 2010), available at www.bloomberg.com/news/articles/2010-10-29/merck-legal-costs-for-vioxx-reduce-profit-6-years-after-recall.

92. Rita Rubin, *How Did Vioxx Debacle Happen?* USAToday.com (Oct. 12, 2004), available at http://usatoday30.usatoday.com/news/health/2004-10-12-vioxx-cover_x.htm.

93. Matthew Herper, *Merck Could Return to Greatness if CEO Can Leave His Own Past Behind*, Forbes.com (April 17, 2013), available at www.forbes.com/sites/matthewherper/2013/04/17/merck-could-return-to-greatness-if-ceo-can-leave-his-own-past-behind/2/.

94. Id.

95. *2013 Form 10-K Annual Report*, Merck.com (2013), available at www.merck.com/investors/financials/annual-reports/.

Chapter 3

1. This quotation came from a personal conversation between Professor Fort and the leaders of a government agency, but the identity of the speaker and the agency must be withheld because of confidentiality requirements.

2. Timothy Fort, personal interview with Jeff Fettig.

3. Raymond Baumhart, *An Honest Profit: What Businessmen Say about Ethics* (1968).

4. Id. at xv.

5. The Corporate Executive Board is a worldwide best practices and consulting organization for business. It has long had a particular interest in issues pertaining to compliance and ethics.

6. Ryan Ulbrich, "5 Trends from 10 years of Surveying Corporate Compliance & Ethics," CEBGlobal.com (August, 2014), available at www.cebglobal.com/blogs/5-trends-from-10-years-of-surveying-corporate-compliance-ethics/.

7. Id.

8. See, for example, *U.S. Sentencing Guidelines Manual* (1984).

9. Ulbrich, *supra* note 6.

10. The authors would like to acknowledge several students from Professor Fort's business ethics classes at the Kelly School of Business. Although the authors drafted initial summaries of the following cases, students also wrote additional research papers that added significantly to the richness of the material and provided awareness of multiple sources that went beyond the initial drafts. All the following material comes from our own distilling of these papers along with our own research, but we are very grateful for this work and the teaching these students did for their teacher and for this book. Thus, we would like to acknowledge Madeline Prehm, Brennan Keough, Benny Nahrstadt, Michael Swilik, Colin Webb, Katie Greulich, Rob Porter, Garrett Lee, Charlie Schubach, Elizabeth Geotz, Elizabeth Kerr, Kelsie Mulvehill, Rachel Turner, Andrew Hensel, Kendall Kleer, Laurie Sites, Jackie Yeh, MacKenzie Conrad, Natasha Mohney, Ali Matisko, Boming Xu, Ruge Shen, Derek Li, Andrew Capshew, Blake Klenovich, Zack Runk, Max Baren, Rachael Pearson, Austin Foote, Brian Wilhite, Pat Stemle, Jian Zheng, Michael Russell, Mary Beth King, Sandy Lam, Eduardo

Sader, Carlos Zambrano, Sicong Ye, Kegao Huang, Yunsheng Yao, Hanbring Yao, Matthew Dunn, Laura Lueken, Emily Murphy, and a student who wished to remain anonymous.

11. Thayer Watkins, "The Rise and Fall of Enron," San Diego State Department of Economics, retrieved on February 17, 2016, from www.sjsu.edu/faculty/watkins/enron.htm.

12. Bethany Mclean, "Fortune Archive: Is Enron Overpriced?" *CNNMoney* (Jan. 19, 2006), available at http://money.cnn.com/2006/01/13/news/companies/enronoriginal_fortune/.

13. Timothy Egan, "Tapes Show Enron Arranged Plant Shutdown," NYTimes.com (Feb. 4, 2005), available at www.nytimes.com/2005/02/04/us/tapes-show-enron-arranged-plant-shutdown.html?_r=0.

14. Bethany McLean & Peter Elkind, "The Guiltiest Guys in the Room," Money.CNN.com (July 5, 2006), available at http://money.cnn.com/2006/05/29/news/enron_guiltyest/.

15. "Market Cap to Maximum Sentence: Booking Enron by the Numbers," WSJ.com (May 25, 2006), available at www.wsj.com/articles/SB114780226218554397.

16. Chris Seabury, "Enron: The Fall of a Wall Street Darling," Investopedia.com, retrieved on January 30, 2016, from www.investopedia.com/articles/stocks/09/enron-collapse.asp.

17. "Market Cap," *supra* note 15.

18. Id.

19. Zeke Ashton, "Cree's Conference Call Blues," The Motley Fool (Oct. 24, 2003), available at www.fool.com/investing/general/2003/10/24/crees-conference-call-blues.aspx.

20. Associated Press, "Former Enron Boss Kenneth Lay Pleads Innocent in Corruption Case," Augusta Times (July 9, 2004), available at http://chronicle.augusta.com/stories/2004/07/09/bus_421553.shtml#.VtXVcpwrKUk.

21. Steven L. Schwarcz, "Enron and the Use and Abuse of Special Purpose Entities in Corporate Structures," 70 University of Cincinnati L. Rev. 1309 (2006).

22. William C. Powers Jr., Raymond S. Troubh, & Herbert S. Winokur Jr., *Report of Investigation by the Special Investigative Committee of the Board of Directors of Enron Corp.* (2002), available at http://i.cnn.net/cnn/2002/LAW/02/02/enron.report/powers.report.pdf.

23. Leslie Wayne, *Enron's Collapse: Before Debacle, Enron Insiders Cashed out $1.1 Billion in Shares*, NYTimes.com (January 13, 2002), available at www.nytimes.com/2002/01/13/business/enron-s-collapse-before-debacle-enron-insiders-cashed-in-1.1-billion-in-shares.html?pagewanted=all.

24. *Martha Stewart—American Entrepreneur and Television Personality.* Encyclopedia Britannica Online, retrieved on January 18, 2016 from www .britannica.com/biography/Martha-Stewart.

25. Jessica Erickson, *Corporate Misconduct and the Perfect Storm of Shareholder Litigation,* 84 Notre Dame Law Review 75, 83–86.

26. Complaint in *Securities Exchange Commission v. Martha Stewart and Peter Baconovic,* filed June 4, 2003, in the United States District Court for the Southern District of New York.

27. Id.

28. Id.

29. Christopher Matthews, *25 Years Later: In the Crash of 1987, the Seeds of the Great Recession,* CNN.com (Oct. 22 2012), available at http://business.time .com/2012/10/22/25-years-later-in-the-crash-of-1987-the-seeds-of-the-great -recession/.

30. Id.

31. Id.

32. *Case Study: The Collapse of Lehman Brothers,* Investopedia.com, retrieved on February 21, 2016, from www.investopedia.com/articles/economics/09 /lehman-brothers-collapse.asp.

33. Id.

34. Louise Story & Eric Dash, *Lehman Channeled Risks Through "Alter Ego" Firm,* NYTimes.com (April 12, 2010), available at www.nytimes .com/2010/04/13/business/13lehman.html?pagewanted=2&hp.

35. *Case Study, supra* note 32.

36. NYU, *The Ford-Firestone case* (2000), available at www.stern.nyu.edu/om /faculty/zemel/ford_firestone.pdf.

37. Id. at 3.

38. Id. at 1.

39. Id. at 11.

40. Id. at 12.

41. Id.

42. Id.

43. Id.

44. Id. at 3.

45. Id. at 6.

46. Id.

47. Id. at 7–8.

48. Id. at 13.

49. *All About Lean* (June 1, 2014);, available at www.allaboutlean.com /toyota-gm-recalls/.

50. Id.

51. Id.

52. Nick Bunkley, *GM Was Reluctant to Recall 1.2 Million Vehicles for Airbag Issue*, AutomotiveNews.com (April 29, 2014), available at www.autonews.com/article/20140429/OEM11/140429850/gm-was-reluctant-to-recall-1.2-million-vehicles-for-airbag-issue.

53. *Toyota "Unintended Acceleration" Has Killed 89*, CBSNews.com (May 25, 2010); available at www.cbsnews.com/news/toyota-unintended-acceleration-has-killed-89/.

54. Reuters, *BP CEO Apologizes for "Thoughtless" Oil Spill Comment*, Reuters.com (June 2, 2010), available at www.reuters.com/article/us-oil-spill-bp-apology-idUSTRE6515NQ20100602.

55. National Commission on the BP Deepwater Horizon Oil Spill and Offshore Drilling, *Deep Water: The Gulf Oil Disaster and the Future of Offshore Drilling* (2010).

56. Campbell Robertson, John Schwartz, & Richard Perez-Pena, *BP to Pay Gulf Coast States $18.7 Billion for Deepwater Horizon Oil Spill*, NYTimes.com (July 2, 2015), available at www.nytimes.com/2015/07/03/us/bp-to-pay-gulf-coast-states-18-7-billion-for-deepwater-horizon-oil-spill.html?_r=0.

Chapter 4

1. See, for example, *In re Johnson and Johnson Derivative Litigation*, Civil Action No. 10-2033 (FLW), N.J. District Court (2011).

2. In 1982, Professor Fort was a third-year law student at Northwestern University in Chicago, living one block north of a Walgreen's store. One fall day, he wasn't feeling well and discovered that he was out of his preferred pain reliever, Extra Strength Tylenol, so he put on his jacket to get more at the Walgreens. It was a nasty day, and his housemate told him to wait until he checked to see if he had something else in his medicine cabinet. He did, and so Fort did not go to the Walgreens. An unlucky flight attendant from United Airlines, however, did go to that same Walgreens that same afternoon, bought Extra Strength Tylenol, and subsequently died. Suffice it to say, the Tylenol case struck close to home!

3. See, for example, Associated Press, *Chicago Tylenol Murders Remain Unsolved after More Than 30 Years*, FoxNews.com (Sept. 28, 2013), available at www.foxnews.com/us/2013/09/28/chicago-tylenol-murders-remain-unsolved-after-more-than-30-years.html.

4. *Our Credo*, Johnson & Johnson, retrieved on February 22, 2016, from www.jnj.com/sites/default/files/pdf/jnj_ourcredo_english_us_8.5x11_cmyk.pdf. The Credo reads as follows:

We believe our first responsibility is to the doctors, nurses and patients, to mothers and fathers and all others who use our products and services. In meeting their needs everything we do must be of high quality. We must constantly strive to reduce our costs in order to maintain reasonable prices. Customers' orders must be serviced promptly and accurately. Our suppliers and distributors must have an opportunity to make a fair profit.

We are responsible to our employees, the men and women who work with us throughout the world. Everyone must be considered as an individual. We must respect their dignity and recognize their merit. They must have a sense of security in their jobs. Compensation must be fair and adequate, and working conditions clean, orderly and safe. We must be mindful of ways to help our employees fulfill their family obligations. Employees must feel free to make suggestions and complaints. There must be equal opportunity for employment, development and advancement for those qualified. We must provide competent management, and their actions must be just and ethical.

We are responsible to the communities in which we live and work and to the world community as well. We must be good citizens—support good works and charities and pay our fair share of taxes. We must encourage civic improvements and better health and education. We must maintain in good order the property we are privileged to use, protecting the environment and natural resources.

Our final responsibility is to our stockholders. Business must make a sound profit. We must experiment with new ideas. Research must be carried on, innovative programs developed and mistakes paid for. New equipment must be purchased, new facilities provided and new products launched. Reserves must be created to provide for adverse times. When we operate according to these principles, the stockholders should realize a fair return.

5. The authors would like to acknowledge several students from Professor Fort's business ethics classes at the Kelly School of Business. Although the authors drafted initial summaries of the following cases, students also wrote additional research papers, which added significantly to the richness of the material and provided awareness of multiple sources that went beyond the initial drafts. All the following material comes from our own distilling of these papers along with our own research, but we are very grateful for this work and the teaching these students did for their teacher and for this book. Thus, we would like to acknowledge Tayler Fisher, Paige Mahrenholz, Stephanie Schneider, Christian Matkovic, Agatha Stopnicki, Kristen Lee, Beth Queisser, Brian Wojciechowski, Spencer Horwitz, Nathan Mulloney, Ryan Mersch, and Chad Rudden (who wrote about the Blue Bell case); Sabrina Alvarez, Ian Boyd, Matt Clements, Julianne Howell, Rebecca Brougher, Lydia Ertel, Adam Jeffrey, and Dan Sigerich (who wrote about the Mattel case); Andrea Martinez, Peiyan Cair, Junyan Lei, Yuhe Pan, Zhirwan Gong, and a student who chose to remain anonymous

(who wrote about the Starbucks case); and Oliveia Sobieraj (who wrote about Maersk).

6. Louise Story & David Barboza, *Mattell Recalls 19 Million Toys Sent from China*, NYTimes.com (August 15, 2007), available at www.nytimes .com/2007/08/15/business/worldbusiness/15imports.html?pagewanted=all/.

7. Id.; see also *Mattell CEO: "Rigorous Standards" after Massive Toy Recall*, CNN.com (Nov. 15, 2007), available at www.cnn.com/2007/US/08/14/recall /index.html.

8. Christopher Palmeri, *What Went Wrong at Mattel*, Bloomberg.com (Aug. 14, 2007), available at www.bloomberg.com/bw/stories/2007-08-14/what-went -wrong-at-mattelbusinessweek-business-news-stock-market-and-financial-advice.

9. "Mattell CEO," *supra* note 7.

10. Id.

11. Tuck School of Business, *Mattel, Inc: The Lead Paint Recall* (2010), re-trieved on February 24, 2016, from http://digitalstrategies.tuck.dartmouth.edu /cds-uploads/case-studies/pdf/MattelRecall6-0033_1.pdf.

12. Id.

13. Story & Barboza, *supra* note 6.

14. Eric S. Lipton & David Barboza, *As More Toys Are Recalled, Trail Ends in China*, New York Times (June 19, 2007).

15. Story & Barboza, *supra* note 6.

16. Mindy Fetterman, Greg Farrell, & Laura Petrecca, *Recall of China-Made Toys Unnerves Parents*, ABCNews.com (Aug. 6, 2007), available at http://abc news.go.com/Business/story?id=3443625.

17. Story & Barboza, *supra* note 6.

18. Ben Blanchard, *Mattel Apologizes to China for Toy Recalls*, Reuters .com (Sept. 21, 2007), available at http://in.reuters.com/article/us-china-safety -mattel-idINPEK10394020070921.

19. *Mattel, Fisher-Price to Pay $2.3 Million Civil Penalty for Violating Federal Lead Paint Ban*, Consumer Product Safety Commission (June 5, 2009), avail-able at www.cpsc.gov/en/Newsroom/News-Releases/2009/Mattel-Fisher-Price -to-Pay-23-Million-Civil-Penalty-for-Violating-Federal-Lead-Paint-Ban-Penalty -is-highest-ever-for-CPSC-regulated-product-violations/.

20. *US Captain Rescued from Pirates*, BBC News (April 13, 2009), available at http://news.bbc.co.uk/2/hi/africa/7996087.stm; and Brian Naylor, *Five Days in the Clutches of Pirates*, NPR.org (Oct. 23, 2015), available at www.npr.org /templates/story/story.php?storyId=103224937.

21. Vibeke Vestergård, *A Sustainable Transformation*, Maersk.com (Dec. 4, 2014), available at www.maersk.com/en/people/2014/12/a-sustainable -transformation.

22. Id.

23. Id.

24. Id.

25. *A. P. Moller-Maersk and Strategic Philanthropy*, SRI Portfolio Management (March 25, 2011), available at http://sriportfolio.com/2011/03/25 /a-p-moller-maersk-and-strategic-philantrophy/.

26. Vestergard, *supra* note 21.

27. Paul A. Argenti, *Collaborating with Activists: How Starbucks Works with NGOs*, 47 California Management Review 91, 98 (2004).

28. Id. *at* 100, 106

29. *What Is Fair Trade?*, FairTradeUSA.org, retrieved on February 26, 2016, from https://fairtradeusa.org/what-is-fair-trade.

30. *Fair Trade Standards*, FairTradeUSA.org, retrieved on February 26, 2016, from https://fairtradeusa.org/certification/standards.

31. Argenti, *supra* note 27, *at* 105.

32. Bruce Horovitz, *Starbucks: 99% Ethically Sourced Java*, USAToday.com (April 10, 2015), available at www.usatoday.com/story/money/2015/04/10 /starbucks-fast-food-restaurants-dining-coffee-ethically-sourced/25571937/.

33. Hanna Thomas, *Starbucks and Palm Oil, Wake up and Smell the Coffee*, The Guaradian (Oct. 25, 2015), available at www.theguardian.com/sustainable -business/2015/aug/25/starbucks-palm-oil-campaign-2015-sumofus-consumers -deforestation-commitments.

34. *Starbucks CEO: Can You "Get Big and Stay Small"?* NPR.org (March 28, 2011), available at www.npr.org/2011/03/28/134738487/starbucks-ceo-can -you-get-big-and-stay-small.

35. Id.

36. Howard Schultz, *Excerpt from* Onward, *Starbucks.com* (March 25, 2011), available at www.starbucks.com/onward/excerpt.

37. Id.

38. Celine Marie-Elise Gossner et al., *The Melamine Incident: Implications for International Food and Feed Safety* 117(12) Environmental Health Perspectives 1803–1808 (2009).

39. Yiyun Luo, *When Apology and Product Recall Is Not Enough* (2010), retrieved on February 26, 2016, from scholarlyrepository.miami.edu/cgi /viewcontent.cgi?article=1070&context=oa_theses.

40. Gossner, *supra* note 38, at 1803.

41. Shefali Sharma and Zhang Rou, *China's Dairy Dilemma: The Evolution and Future Trends of China's Dairy Industry* (Feb. 2014), retrieved on February 21, 2016, from www.iatp.org/files/2014_02_25_DairyReport_f_web.pdf.

42. *Timeline: China Milk Scandal*, BBC News (Jan. 25, 2010), available at http://news.bbc.co.uk/2/hi/7720404.stm.

43. *Production Will Begin as Soon as Testing Equipment Is in Place*, Arla .com (Sept. 19, 2008), available at www.arla.com/company/news-and-press /2008/pressrelease/production-will-begin-as-soon-as-testing-equipment-is-in -place-760489/.

44. Luo, *supra* note 39.

45. Id.

46. *Milk Powder Production Resumes in China*, Arla.com (Oct. 16, 2008), available at www.arla.com/company/news-and-press/2008/pressrelease/milk -powder-production-resumes-in-china-760487/.

47. Kelli Levey, *Recipe for Success*, The Bryan-College Station Eagle (June 4, 2004).

48. Jillian Sederholm, *Blue Bell Ice Cream Recall after Listeriosis Linked to Three Deaths*, NBCNews.com (March 14, 2015), available at www.nbcnews .com/news/us-news/blue-bell-ice-cream-linked-deadly-illness-n323396.

49. Caroline Moss, *People Are Trying to Sell Pints of "Listeria-Free" Blue Bell Ice Cream on Craigslist for Thousands of Dollars*, BusinessInsider.com (May 5, 2015), available at www.businessinsider.com/buy-blue-bell-ice-cream-after -listeria-recall-2015-5.

50. *Blue Bell Creameries Voluntarily Expands Recall to Include All of Its Products Due to Possible Health Risk*, Bluebell.com (April 20, 2015), available at www .bluebell.com/the_little_creamery/press_releases/all-product-recall.

51. Laura Lorenzetti, *Blue Bell Creameries Pulls All Its Products over Listeria Risk*, Fortune.com (April 21, 2015), available at http://fortune.com/2015/04/21 /blue-bell-listeria-risk/.

52. Ralph Ellis & Holly Yan, *CDC: Blue Bell Listeria Outbreak Dates to 2010*, CNN.com (April 20, 2015), available at www.cnn.com/2015/04/20/health /blue-bell-ice-cream-recall/.

53. Rick Harmon, *Blue Bell Says Its Ice Cream Won't Return Soon*, USA-Today.com (May 8, 2015), available at www.cnn.com/2015/04/20/health /blue-bell-ice-cream-recall/.

54. Emi Boscamp, *The World's Busiest Airlines*, HuffingtonPost.com (June 18, 2013), available at www.huffingtonpost.com/2013/06/18/busiest-airlines -world_n_3460451.html.

55. David Crouch, *Ryanair Closes Denmark Operation to Head off Union Row*, TheGuardian.com (July 17, 2015), available at www.theguardian .com/business/2015/jul/17/ryanair-closes-denmark-operation-temporarily -to-sidestep-union-dispute.

56. Id.

57. Paul O'Donoghue, *Copenhagen Mayor Bans 45,000 Staff from Flying Ryanair*, Independent.ie (May 19, 2015), available at www.independent.ie

/business/world/copenhagen-mayor-bans-45000-staff-from-flying-ryanair -31233485.html.

58. See Crouch, *supra* note 55.

59. Wayne F. Casico, *Decency Means More than "Always Low Prices": A Comparison of Costco to Wal-Mart's Sam's' Club*, 20(3) Academy of Management Perspectives 26, 31 (2006).

60. Id.

61. One analyst said that it was better to be an employee or customer of Costco than a shareholder. Bruno Dyck & Mitchel Neubert, *Walmart versus Costco: Is Wall Street Ready for Multistream Strategies?* in Management: Current Practice and New Directions (2009) at 17.

62. Steven Greenhouse, *How Costco Became the Anti Wal-Mart*, NYTimes .com (July 17, 2005), available at www.nytimes.com/2005/07/17/business/your money/how-costco-became-the-antiwalmart.html.

63. Id.

64. Id.

Chapter 5

1. Peter Coy, ed., *The Future of Work*, Businessweek (August 2007).

2. Ellen Mignoni, interview for Professor Fort's George Washington University class, March 2012.

3. See, for example, Glyn Richards, *The Philosophy of Gandhi: A Study of His Basic Ideas* (1991.)

4. Sandra L. Robinson & Anne M. O'Leary-Kelly, *Monkey See, Monkey Do: The Influence of Work Groups on the Antisocial Behavior of Employees*, 41 Acadaemy of Management Journal 658.

5. Timothy L. Fort, *The Vision of the Firm: Its Governance, Obligations, and Aspirations* (2014).

6. Illustration based on the work of Danish Psychologist Edgar Rubin, in his two-volume work *Synsoplevede Figurer (Visual Figures)* (1915).

7. Lawrence Kohlberg, *The Philosophy of Moral Development* (1981) at 19.

8. Id.

9. Timothy L. Fort, *The Vision of the Firm*, 2nd ed. (2017).

10. The case continued, in various ways, for many years. The court awarded custody to Mr. Mays, but, less than a year later, Kimberly moved in with her biological parents. That lasted for about two years until she reached the age of 18 and she moved out on her own and was married shortly thereafter. See www .tampabay.com/news/courts/civil/from-the-archives-switched-at-birth-8212 -stories-about-kimberly-mays-from/2255916.

11. Dara Lubarsky, interview for Professor Fort's George Washington University class (2013).

12. See Anjanette Raymond, Timothy L. Fort, & Scott J. Shakelford, *The Angel on Your Shoulder: Prompting Employees to Do the Right Thing Through the Use of Wearables*, Northwestern University Journal of Technology and Intellectual Property (2016).

13. See Robert Prentice, *Teaching Behavioral Ethics*, 31 Journal of Legal Studies Education 325 (2014).

14. See David Messick, Max Bazerman, & Lisa Stewart, *Avoiding Ethical Danger Zones*, available at www.corporate-ethics.org/pdf/danger_zones.pdf; see also Prentice, *supra* note 12.

15. *See*, Messick et al., *supra* note 13; see also Prentice, *supra* note 12.

16 *See* Messick et al., supra note 13; see also Prentice, *supra* note 12.

17. See Prentice, *supra* note 12, at 51.

18. See, generally, Prentice, *supra* note 12.

19. Sarah Schwarzbeck, interview for Professor Fort's George Washington University class (2013).

20. The following discussion of steps 2 through 7 comes from Fort, *supra* note 5.

21. The authors gratefully acknowledge the work of several students from Professor Fort's business ethics class at the Kelley School of Business at Indiana University. Several students wrote research papers on the 2015 Volkswagen situation. Although the authors have written this case on their own, and any mistakes pertaining to the description of the case are ours, we do wish to thank the following students for their good work: MacKenzie Conrad, Natasha Mohney, Andrew Capshew, Blake Klenovich, Zack Runk, Max Baren, Ali Matisko, Booming Xu, Ruge Shen, and Derek Li.

22. Jason Siu, *Top 10 Best Selling Cars of All Time*, AutoGuide.com (Feb. 9, 2012), available at www.autoguide.com/auto-news/2012/02/top-10-best-selling -cars-of-all-time.html.

23. Benjamin Elgin, Dune Lawrence, & Vernon Silver, *How Could Volkswagen's Top Engineers Not Have Known?*, Bloomberg.com (Oct. 21, 2015), available at www.bloomberg.com/news/articles/2015-10-21/how-could-volkswagen-s -top-engineers-not-have-known-.

24. Environmental Protection Agency. News release (September 18, 2015). Available at www.epa.gov/newsreleases/epa-california-notify-volkswagen-clean -air-act-violations-carmaker-allegedly-used.

25. Kalyeena Makortoff, *What You Need to Know about the Volkswagen Scandal*, CNBC.com (Sept. 22, 2015), available at www.cnbc.com/2015/09/22 /what-you-need-to-know-about-the-volkswagen-scandal.html.

26. Jack Ewing & Danielle Ivory. *Volkswagen U.S. Chief Knew of Potential Emissions Problems in 2014*. NYTimes.com (Oct. 7, 2015), available at www .nytimes.com/2015/10/08/business/international/volkswagen-diesel-emissions -fix.html.

27. Marcelo Del Pozo, *Volkswagen CEO Says Emissions Scandal Bill Could Rise*, CNBC.com (Oct. 22, 2015), available at www.cnbc.com/2015/10/22 /emissions-scandal-volkswagen-may-have-to-set-aside-more-funds-if-sales-fall .html.

28. Jack Ewing, *Volkswagen Investigating if Diesel Emissions Deception Was More Extensive*. NYTimes.com (October 22, 2015), available at www.nytimes .com/2015/10/23/business/international/volkswagen-diesel-investigation.html.

29. Lubarsky interview, *supra* note 10.

30. Schwarzbeck interview, *supra* note 18.

31. Reuven Avi-Yonah, *The Cyclical Transformations of the Corporate Form: A Historical Perspective on Corporate Social Responsibility*, 30 Del. J. Corp. L. 767 (2005).

32. Larue T. Hosmer, *Moral Leadership in Business* (1993), at 131.

33. Rawls undertook a thought experiment. Suppose that a person—many persons, really—put themselves behind what he called a veil of ignorance and are in "the original position." In other words, a person knows she will be born, but beyond that doesn't know any of the particular defining characteristics that a human has. The person could be male or female; doesn't know what skin color he will have, whether she is going to be smart or stupid, tall or short, a good athlete or a bad athlete, whether he is going to be musical. She (I purposely use alternating pronouns here because gender identity is one of the unknowns) doesn't know any of those things. He just knows that he is going to be a person.

If you had 100 people in the original position—you can make it 1,000 people, or a million people, or whatever number you want—what kind of deal would they construct for what a fair society would look like?

34. Lubarsky interview, *supra* note 10.

35. Thomas Donaldason & Thomas Dunfee, *Ties that Bind: A Social Contracts Approach to Business Ethics* (1999). To continue with their theory, similarly, Donaldson and Dunfee recognized that one who is applying a moral value needs to give a degree of moral free space so that individual societies and cultures are free to develop their own moral norms. If people in that society consent to that moral norm, then the norm is what they call "authentic." It has some level of credibility. At the same time, Donaldson and Dunfee are not willing to just let everything be relative. Even if people allegedly consent, there still may be some things that violate what they call "cross-cultural hypernorms" that still make certain actions wrong and require some sort of a correction.

Donaldson and Dunfee recognize this as well, so they argue for a sense of moral free space for societies and communities to develop their own moral norms. If people consent to them, fine. That constitutes one level of respect that is due to that society. However, these extant social contracts should still be evaluated according to a larger philosophical social contract that is anchored by hypernorms.

What are those hypernorms? The first answer is that they are something of a work in progress. We will continue to find norms that cut across cultures through additional empirical research. As a provision-holding spot (and this isn't Donaldson and Dunfee's position—this is argument of some of their interpreters), basic rights might well have a lot of overlap with hypernorms.

36. Mignoni interview, *supra* note 2.

Chapter 6

1. R. Jay Magill, *Sincerity: How a Moral Idea Born 500 Years Ago Inspired Religious Wars, Modern Art, Hipster Chic, and the Curious Notion That We All Have Something to Say (No Matter How Dull)* (2012).

2. Georg Wilhelm Friedrich Hegel, *Stanford Encyclopedia of Philosophy* (Feb. 13, 1997; revised August 4, 2015), available at http://plato.stanford.edu/entries/hegel/.

3. Magill, *supra* note 1, at 14.

4. Lionel Trilling, *Sincerity and Authenticity* (1972), at 6.

5. Magill, *supra* note 1, at 22.

6. See Authenticity, *Stanford Encyclopedia of Philosophy* (Sept. 11, 2014), available at http://plato.stanford.edu/entries/Authenticity/.

7. Id.

8. See, for example, Magill, *supra* note 1, at 12:
   Sincerity, after all, is not the same thing as honesty, which means saying what you know to be the truth about objective things or events, regardless of how you feel about them. Sincerity is also not the same as frankness, which means revealing one's judgment about someone or something, even though that judgment might offend. Being sincere is a "rather more tricky state of affairs": it means conforming one's innermost thoughts or emotions and relaying straightforwardly, no matter how relevant to the topic, injurious to one's own reputation, or embarrassing—or however correct or incorrect. Sincerity, in other words, is a subjective state that need not have anything to do with reality.

9. See Authenticity, *supra* note 6.

10. Id.

11. Magill, *supra* note 1, at 206.

12. Id. at 20.

13. See, for example, F. A. Hayek, *The Fatal Conceit: The Errors of Socialism* (1988); and Larue T. Hosmer, *The Ethics of Management* (1987).

14. As we hope the diligent reader has deduced by now, this is essentially the thesis statement the authors are seeking to support.

15. See, for example, *Citizens United v. Federal Election Commission*, 558 U.S. 310 (2010).

16. See, for example, Dan R. Dalton, S. Trevis Certo, & Catherine M. Daily, *Initial Public Offerings as a Web of Conflicts of Interest: An Empirical Assessment*, 13(3) Business Ethics Quarterly 289 (Jul. 2003).

17. Abbey Stemler & Timothy L. Fort, The Ethical Pitfalls and Opportunities of Initial Public Offerings, in *The Challenges of Ethics and Entrepreneurship in the Global Environment (Advances in the Study of Entrepreneurship, Innovation & Economic Growth, Volume 25)* (2015, Sherry Hoskinson and Donald F. Kuratko, eds.), at 39.

18. Id.

19. See, for example, Joshua D. Margolis, Hillary Anger Elfenbein, & James P. Walsh, *Does It Pay to Be Good . . . and Does It Matter? A Meta-Analysis of the Relationship between Corporate Social and Financial Performance* (2009); and Marc Orlitzky, Frank L. Schmidt, & Sara L. Rynes, *Corporate Social and Financial Performance: A Meta-Analysis*, 24(3) Organization Studies 403 (2003).

20. Stemler & Fort, *supra* note 17.

21. See James A. Waters & Frederick Bird, *The Moral Dimension of Organizational Culture*, 6(1) J. Bus. Ethics 15 (1987).

22. See id.

23. *Twenty Years of Positive Change*, Timberland.com, retrieved on February 27, 2016, from http://responsibility.timberland.com/service/20-years-of -positive-change/.

24. The following four paragraphs are adapted from a previous collaboration between the authors: Alexandra Christina, Countess of Fredriksborg, & Timothy L. Fort, *The Paradox of Pharmaceutical CSR*, Bus. Horizons 151 (March–April 2014).

25. Alexandra Christina, Countess of Fredriksborg, *The Essence of Trust in Business Today*, speech presented at the 2012 Business for Peace Summit, Oslo, Norway.

26. This section is adapted from a previous collaboration between the authors: Alexandra Christina, Countess of Fredriksborg, & Timothy L. Fort, *Catalyst, Obstacle, or Something in Between? Dealing with the Law in Building Ethical Corporate Culture*, 29 Notre Dame J. L. Ethics & Pub. Pol'y 1 (2015).

27. Id.

28. See, for example, Elliott D. Cohen, *You Are a Social Animal*, Psychology Today (Sept. 21, 2010), available at www.psychologytoday.com/blog

/what-would-aristotle-do/201009/you-are-social-animal (citing to the works of Aristotle).

29. See, for example, Paul Lawrence & Jay W. Lorsch, *Differentiation and Integration in Complex Organizations*, 12(1) Administrative Science Quarterly 1 (June 1967).

30. *See* Timothy L. Fort, *Ethics and Governance* (2001).

31. Id. at 49–51.

32. Dunbar has other examples as well. He goes on to note that the Mormons followed a pattern similar to the Hutterites, writing that when Brigham Young led the Mormons to Utah, he divided his flock of 5,000 into groups of 150. Dunbar also reports that a study conducted by the Church of England found that the ideal congregation size is less than 200 and that, over the past hundred years, the military company unit has ranged from 130 (the number in Gandhi's ashram) to 170. These anthropological realities suggest that certain capacities are universal among human beings. The findings themselves do not suggest universal norms but do indicate basic human capacities that may have an impact on how human beings relate to each other. Id. at 21; see also Robin Dunbar, *Gossip, Grooming, and the Evolution of Language* (1996).

33. See Fort, *supra* note 30.

Chapter 7

1. Interview by Timothy Fort with Bob Jones, CEO of Old National Bank, on December 11, 2015.

2. Id.

Index

stock prices, 50, 51, 52, 59, 74, 109
Stockton, Bryan, 65
Stora Enso, 10
subprime home loan market, 51
Swiss Re, 10

Tanzania, 15
Taylor, Charles: on authenticity, 106
techno-symbolic values, 27, 28, 33
telecommunications industry:
   compliance programs in, 40
Third World countries: medicines
   contributed to, 4
Timberland, 10, 109, 114
Toyota: relationship with General
   Motors, 22–23; "sticking" accelerator
   scandal, 46, 53, 54, 57, 58
toy recalls, 64–65, 92, 103
trade: embargoes, 7; Hayek on, 4–5,
   7–8, 127n4
Transfair USA, 69
Transocean, 55
Treviño, Linda, 13; *Ethical Decision
   Making in Organizations*, 29
Trilling, Lionel: on sincerity, 106
Trump, Donald, 9
trust, 6, 17, 41, 47, 84, 89, 107; good
   trust, 18, 34, 37; hard trust, 18,
   33–34, 37; instrumental view of,
   35–36; mention in IPO documents,
   110; as model of business ethics,
   26–27; real trust, 18, 35–37;
   relationship to authenticity, 108;
   relationship to business performance,
   22, 108–9, 110, 118; relationship
   to integrity, 18, 23; relationship
   to law, 26–27, 122; relationship
   to leadership, 38; relationship to
   sincerity, 19, 32, 37, 108, 116, 117;
   undermining of, 21
truthfulness, 106, 107, 116
Turing Pharmaceutical, 13; CEO
   Shredi, 9; and price of Daraprim,
   8–9, 87, 94
Twigg, Ernest and Regina, 87–88

Tylenol recall, 5–6, 21, 47, 60–63, 64,
   66, 92, 103, 140n2. *See also* Johnson
   & Johnson

UN Declaration on Human Rights,
   126
United Auto Workers Union (UAW),
   22–23
United Nations Environment
   Programme, 14
U.S. Federal Sentencing Guidelines, 34;
   1991 amendments, 12
U.S. Senate: Finance Committee, 36
U.S. Supreme Court: *Burlington
   Industries v. Ellerth*, 12
utilitarianism and stakeholder theory,
   98, 102–3

values: as competing, 26, 27, 28,
   135n54, 135n55; ecologizing values,
   26, 27, 28; economizing values, 26,
   27, 28; power-aggrandizing values,
   26–27, 28; of shareholders, 5–6, 95,
   96–97; techno-symbolic values, 27,
   28, 33; values-based management,
   35–36, 37, 114–15; values-driven
   governance, 19; x-factor values, 27,
   28, 30. *See also* ethics
Vidaver-Cohen, Deborah: *Moral
   Climate in Business Firms*, 29
Vioxx scandal, 33, 36
virtues: accountability, 42, 43, 58, 59,
   63, 75, 78, 104, 116, 118; ambition,
   43; as applied to problematic cases,
   58, 75; CEOs on, 42, 43, 46, 58,
   59, 62–63, 75, 78, 104, 107, 109,
   120; creativity, 42, 43; decision
   making and virtue theory, 91,
   103–4; efficiency, 43; excellence, 90;
   as exhibited in exemplary cases, 75,
   78; and group size, 116; honesty,
   42, 43, 44, 58, 59, 63, 75, 78, 90,
   104, 116, 118; integrity, 42, 43, 44,
   58, 59, 63, 75, 78, 90, 118; loyalty,
   42, 43, 58, 59, 63, 75, 78, 118;